Paul's Journey
FROM
TARSUS
TO
ROME

To order additional copies of
Paul's Jouney From Tarsus to Rome,
by Rex D. Edwards, call **1-800-765-6955.**

Visit us at **www.reviewandherald.com** for information on
other Review and Herald® products.

Paul's Journey

FROM
TARSUS
TO
ROME

To live is Christ.

REX D. EDWARDS

REVIEW AND HERALD® PUBLISHING ASSOCIATION
Since 1861 | www.reviewandherald.com

Published by Review and Herald® Publishing Association, Hagerstown, MD 21741-1119

Review and Herald® titles may be purchased in bulk for educational, business, fund-raising, or sales promotional use. For information, e-mail SpecialMarkets@reviewandherald.com.

The Review and Herald® Publishing Association publishes biblically based materials for spiritual, physical, and mental growth and Christian discipleship.

The author assumes full responsibility for the accuracy of all facts and quotations as cited in this book.

Texts credited to ASV are from *The Holy Bible,* edited by the American Revision Committee, Standard Edition, Thomas Nelson & Sons, 1901.

Scripture quotations marked ESV are from *The Holy Bible*, English Standard Version, copyright © 2001 by Crossway Bibles, a division of Good News Publishers. Used by permission. All rights reserved.

Texts credited to NEB are from *The New English Bible.* © The Delegates of the Oxford University Press and the Syndics of the Cambridge University Press 1961, 1970. Reprinted by permission.

Texts credited to NIV are from the *Holy Bible, New International Version*. Copyright © 1973, 1978, 1984, 2011 by Biblica, Inc. Used by permission. All rights reserved worldwide.

Texts credited to NKJV are from the New King James Version. Copyright © 1979, 1980, 1982 by Thomas Nelson, Inc. Used by permission. All rights reserved.

Bible texts credited to Phillips are from J. B. Phillips: *The New Testament in Modern English,* Revised Edition. © J. B. Phillips 1958, 1960, 1972. Used by permission of Macmillan Publishing Co.

Bible texts credited to RSV are from the Revised Standard Version of the Bible, copyright © 1946, 1952, 1971, by Division of Christian Education of the National Council of the Churches of Christ in the U.S.A. Used by permission.

This book was
Edited by Vesna Mirkovich
Copyedited by Megan Mason
Cover photo and design by Ron J. Pride/Review and Herald® Design Center
Interior design by Derek Knecht/Review and Herald® Design Center
Typeset: Minion Pro 11/13

PRINTED IN U.S.A.

18 17 16 15 14   5 4 3 2 1

Library of Congress Cataloging-in-Publication Data
Edwards, Rex.
  Paul's journey from Tarsus to Rome : to live is Christ / Rex D. Edwards.
      pages cm
  Includes bibliographical references and index.
  ISBN 978-0-8280-2712-0 (alk. paper)
1. Paul, the Apostle, Saint. 2. Apostles--Biography. I. Title.
  BS2506.3.E36 2014
  225.9'2--dc23
  [B]
                             2013016999
ISBN 978-0-8280-2712-0

Dedicated

To my beloved son,
Dr. L. Paul Edwards, who, like his apostolic namesake,
in the deep silence of adversity has exhibited indefatigable
strength, and, with Shakespeare, can say,
"Then know, that I have little wealth to lose;
A man I am cross'd with adversity."*

———————

Two Gentlemen of Verona, Act IV, scene 1, lines 11, 12.

Contents

Introduction

James Stalker writes:

"There are some men whose lives it is impossible to study without receiving the impression that they were expressly sent into the world to do a work required by the juncture of history on which they fell. The story of the Reformation, for example, cannot be read by a devout mind without wonder at the providence by which such great men as Luther, Zwingli, Calvin, and Knox were simultaneously raised by in different parts of Europe to break the yoke of the papacy and republish the gospel of grace. . . . This impression is produced by no life more than that by the apostle Paul."[1]

Adolf von Harnack adds: "What missionary is there, what preacher, what man entrusted with the cure of souls, who can be compared with him, whether in the greatness of the task he accomplished, or in the holy energy with which he carried it out."[2]

Yet Paul's appearance, according to tradition, was hideous. His stature was not impressive, but his body was strong and well-sculpted and broad, and even the bowed legs added to that impression of vigorous strength. He was like some primitive fire god, with that raised and crested mane of intensely red hair, with those red eyebrows almost meeting above his eyes, and the virile low forehead and the pointed, Vulcan-like ears. No soft grace or elegance, but only an aura of power. Saul's features—the wide, thin lips; the great nose; the hard, firm chin—spoke of power.

"At times he looked like a man," reports W. M. Ramsey, "and at times he had the face of an angel."[3] The sixth-century Byzantine historian John Maladas adds that he had a thick gray beard, light-blue eyes, and a fair and florid complexion, and that he was a man who often smiled. Nicephorus Callistus, in the fourteenth century, noted further that Paul's beard was rather pointed, that his large nose was handsomely curved, and that his body was slight and rather bent. Are these traditions true? Thomas Arnold warned, "I am well satisfied that if you let in but one little finger of tradition, you will have in the whole monster-horns and tale and all." What is more important than knowing what he really looked like is to understand the nature of his mission and why he was known as the apostle to the Gentiles.

One of Christ's missions was to break down the wall of separation between Jew and Gentile and make the blessings of salvation the property of all people, irrespective of race or language. However, He was not permitted to bring about this change, for He was cut off in the midst of His days and had to leave this task to His followers.

Before Paul appeared on the scene, Peter had already begun to lay the foundation of Paul's divine task by admitting the first Gentiles into the church by baptism. Then came Stephen. He met his death for declaring the universality of God's kingdom, that Christianity was destined to spread the blessing of salvation far beyond the Jewish race, even over the whole world; and his dying prayer received its fulfillment in the conversion of one who, being the apostle of the Gentiles, labored most to preach the gospel to "every creature which is under heaven." Augustine said, "If Stephen had not prayed, Paul would never have been given to the church."[4] Indeed, as P. C. Ainsworth portrays, Stephen's death proved to be a portal for the gospel message:

"And the stones that bruised him and struck him down
Shone dazzling gems in his victor's crown;
And as his spirit fled,
A light from the land where the angels dwell

Lingered saintly and grand where the martyr fell."

So Paul gave his heart to the Gentile mission. In him, Jesus Christ went forth to evangelize the world. Paul's versatility and education enabled him to encounter rabbis in their synagogues, proud magistrates in their courts, and philosophers in their haunts of learning; he was one who could cut his way out of the jungle of the peculiarities and prejudices of Jewish exclusiveness.

Paul was born about the same time as Jesus. This can be deduced from the fact that Stephen was stoned in the year A.D. 33 and that Paul was a "young man" (Acts 7:58, NKJV) at the time. In the Greek world this could mean that Paul was anywhere from 20 to 30 years of age. In this case "young man" probably meant the latter, since he was a member of the Sanhedrin, an office no one who was under 30 years of age could hold.

Further, the commission to persecute the Christians would scarcely have been entrusted to a particularly young man. In A.D. 62, about 30 years after playing this sad, integral part in Stephen's murder, Paul was lying in a Roman prison awaiting the death sentence for the same cause for which Stephen had suffered, and, writing one of the last of his epistles (Philemon), he called himself an old man. When the boy Jesus was playing in the streets of Nazareth, the boy Paul was playing in the streets of his native town of Tarsus, away on the other side of the ridges of Lebanon.

About halfway between Jerusalem, the home of Judaism, and Constantinople, the capital of the first Christian emperor of Rome, stood Tarsus, the birthplace and early home of that man who, more than any other, carried Christianity from Judea throughout the Roman Empire. George Holley Gilbert writes in *The Student's Life of Paul*: "The city was in level Cilicia, 60 miles west of the field where Alexander defeated Darius (333

B.C.), 129 miles west of Antioch, the first metropolis of Gentile Christianity, and 515 miles northwest of Jerusalem. It was situated on the Cydnus River, 12 miles from the Mediterranean coast, for which distance was navigable in Paul's time. It was called the capital of Cilicia when Cicero was governor of the province (51-50 B.C.), and later bore the title of *metropolis.*"[5]

At the time of Paul's arrest in Jerusalem and imprisonment in Caesarea, Felix, the Roman procurator, received the prisoner and at once asked to what province he belonged, and he was informed that he was from Cilicia.

"Tarsus, the chief city of Cilicia," says F. F. Bruce, "was now about a thousand years old. It had been subject in turn to the Assyrians, Persians, and Graeco-Macedonians. It received a civic constitution from Antiochus IV in 171 B.C. and ranked Free city under the Romans from 64 B.C. onwards. It was one of the three leading centers of learning in the world of those days. Its schools were devoted to philosophy, rhetoric and law."[6]

Tarsus, whom the inhabitants called "the Pearl of the Cydnus River," was essentially a Phoenician city. Hellenistic in attitude, though Eastern in emotion, it was famed for its craftsmen, enriched by its pirates. Many were the natives who proudly called themselves "a little Rome"; a score of races lived there, and the narrow streets clamored with a multitude of tongues.

The town enjoyed an extensive trade in the long, fine goats' hair, used to make a coarse kind of cloth for manufacturing various articles. Among these goods manufactured and merchandised all along the Mediterranean shores were tents, such as the ones Paul would have been employed to fabricate. Tarsus was also the center of a large transport trade, for behind the town a famous pass, called the Cilician Gates, led up through the Taurus Mountains to the central countries of Asia Minor;

and Tarsus was the depot to which the products of these countries were brought down to be distributed over the East and the West.

Students from many countries were seen in its streets. It rivaled Athens and Alexandria, two university cities, in intellectual eminence. Was not Tarsus a fit birthplace for this apostle to the Gentiles?

During his ministry Paul was always a lover of cities. Whereas Jesus avoided Jerusalem and loved to teach on the mountainside or the lakeshore, Paul was constantly moving from one great city to another. Antioch, Ephesus, Athens, Corinth, Rome, the capitals of the ancient world, were the scenes of his activity. The words of Jesus were redolent of the country and teem with pictures of its still beauty—the lilies of the field, the sheep following the shepherd, the sower in the furrow, the fishermen drawing their nets. But the language of Paul is impregnated with the atmosphere of the city, with the tramp and hurry of the streets: the soldier in full armor, the athlete in the arena, the building of houses and temples, the triumphal procession of the victorious general.

Paul had a certain pride in the place of his birth, evidenced by his boasting on one occasion that he was a citizen of no mean city. Yet he was an alien in the land of his birth. His father was one of the numerous Jews who were scattered over the cities of the Gentile world, engaged in trade and commerce. They had left the Holy Land, but they had not forgotten it. They never coalesced with the populations among which they dwelt; in dress, food, and religion they remained a peculiar people. It is probable that his father had not left Palestine before his son's birth, for Paul calls himself a Hebrew of the Hebrews—a name that belonged only to the Palestinian Jews. So the land and city of Paul's heart were Palestine and Jerusalem; and the heroes of his young imagination were not Curtius and Horatius, Hercules and Achilles, but Abraham and Joseph, Moses and David and Ezra.

Did Paul attend the University of Tarsus? Did he drink at the wells of wisdom that flow from Mount Helicon before he went to sit by those that spring from Mount Zion? It may be inferred from Paul's reference to the Greek poets that he was acquainted with Greek literature. His speech at Athens shows that he was able to wield a style much more stately than that of his writings. Further, the University of Tarsus was famous for debates and rivalries, and such windy disputations form a marked feature in some of his writings.

The college for the education of Jewish rabbis was in Jerusalem, and Paul was about 13 years of age when he was sent there. His arrival in the Holy City may have happened in the same year in which Jesus, at the age of 12, first visited it. To every Jewish child of a religious disposition, Jerusalem was the center of all things; the footsteps of the prophets and kings echoed in the streets, and memories sacred and sublime cling to its walls and buildings.

A most noteworthy teacher presided over the college of Jerusalem at that time: Gamaliel, at whose feet Paul tells us he was brought up. Gamaliel's contemporaries called him the Beauty of the Law, and the Jews still remember him as the Great Rabbi. He was a Pharisee strongly attached to the traditions of the fathers, yet not intolerant or hostile to Greek culture, as some of the narrower Pharisees were. The influence of this man is evident in Paul's theology and ministry.

The course of a rabbi's instruction consisted entirely of the study of the Scriptures and the respective commentary the sages supplied. Students would commit to memory the words of Scripture and the sayings of their wise, and carry out discussions about disputed points. Paul's marvelous memory and keenness of logic conspicuous in his ministry demonstrate the importance of this training.

Although he was to be specially the missionary to the Gentiles, he was also a great missionary to his own people. Whenever he visited a city with Jewish inhabitants, his first public appearance would be in the synagogue, where his rabbinic training and knowledge of the Old Testament secured him an opportunity to speak. Besides, he was destined to be the greatest theologian of Christianity, and the principal writer of the New Testament.

What happened to Paul after he completed his studies in Jerusalem? Did he return to his native Cilicia? Did he hold office in some synagogue there? At all events he was for some years at a distance from Jerusalem and Palestine, for these were the years of John the Baptist and the ministry of Jesus.

Yet only 2 or 3 years old, Christianity was growing very quietly in Jerusalem. Those who had heard its message at Pentecost carried the news to their homes in many quarters. At first the authorities were inclined to persecute it, but they changed their minds and, acting under the advice of Gamaliel, resolved to neglect it, believing that it would die out if left alone. The Christians, on the other hand, gave as little offense as possible; in the externals of religion they continued to be strict Jews and zealous of the law, attending the Temple worship and observing the Jewish ceremonies. It was a kind of truce, which allowed Christianity a little space for secret growth.

But the truce could not last; it was soon to be invaded with terror and bloodshed. The new wine of gospel liberty was to burst the flasks of Jewish law.

Throughout this book we will follow in the footsteps of

the most passionate, intelligent, urban, and dedicated apostle of early Christianity, Saul of Tarshish, or, as the Romans called him, Paul of Tarsus, the intellectual Pharisee and lawyer and theologian, and, finally, the apostle to the Gentiles. As Udo Schnelle observes, "Paul's life was the life of a traveler. Like no other before or after him, he bridged different continents, cultures, and religions and created a new continuing reality: Christianity as a world religion."[7]

On this journey we will realize that humankind, as a whole, never really changes, in that the problems of Saul's world are the same that confront us today. George Santanaya, influenced by pre-Christian philosophers such as Socrates, Plato, and Aristotle, said that "those who do not remember the past are doomed to repeat it."

---

[1] James Stalker, *The Life of St. Paul* (Edinburgh: T & T Clark, n.d.), p. 11.

[2] Adolf von Harnack, *What Is Christianity?* trans. Thomas Biley Saunders (New York: Harper & Row, 1900, 1957), p. 188.

[3] W. M. Ramsay, *The Church in the Roman Empire* (London: G. P. Putnam's Sons, 1893), p. 32; cf. M. R. James, *The Apocryphal New Testament* (Oxford: Claredon Press, 1924), p. 273.

[4] *Ibid.*

[5] George Holley Gilbert, *The Student's Life of Paul* (New York: MacMillan, 1902), p.1.

[6] F. F. Bruce, *The Book of Acts* (Grand Rapids: Eerdmans, 1974), pp. 207, 208.

[7] Udo Schnelle, *Apostle Paul: His Life and Theology* (Grand Rapids: Baker Academic, 2006), p. 25.

1 DAMASCUS:
PERSECUTOR TO PROCLAIMER

"As he journeyed, he came near to Damascus" (Acts 9:3).

The group of horsemen galloping on the road to Damascus was halted quicker than a bombshell ever halted a Humvee on a Baghdad road. The Syrian noonday, because of the clarity of the atmosphere, was the brightest of all middays and terrific for brilliance. But suddenly in that noon there flashed from the heavens a light that made that Syrian sun seem as tame as a star in comparison. It was the face of the slain and ascended Christ looking from the heavens, and under the dash of that overpowering light, all the horses dropped, along with their riders—human face and horse's mane together in the dust. And then two claps of thunder following, uttering the epizeuxis: "Saul! Saul!" For three days that fallen equestrian was totally blind. What cornea and crystalline lens could endure brightness greater than the noonday Syrian sun?

I had read it a hundred times, but it never so impressed me before and probably will never so impress me again as when I stood before the equestrian statue of Saul that fronts the Church of St. Paul near the west gate that leads into the city of Damascus. I read the familiar narrative: "As he neared Damascus on his journey, suddenly a light from heaven flashed around him. He fell to the ground and heard a voice say to him, 'Saul, Saul, why do you persecute me?' 'Who are you, Lord?' Saul asked. 'I am Jesus, whom you are persecuting'" (Acts 9:3-6, NIV). The road from Jerusalem to Damascus has for thousands of years taken cavalcades of mounted officers on its dusty path. It was a long journey of more than 160 miles; and with the slow means of locomotion then available, it would occupy at least six days. Now on this very road a fierce little man, who made up by magnitude of hatred for Christianity for his diminutive stature, was the leading spirit. Though suffering from chronic inflammation of the eyes, yet from those eyes flashed more indignation against Christ's followers than any one of the horsed procession. This little man, before his name was changed to Paul, was called Saul. We will meet this unhorsed equestrian later in Damascus, toward which his horse's head is turned.

The city of Damascus, believed by the Arabs to be the oldest continuously inhabited city in the world and built by Noah's grandson, was always a province or an empire. It was called "the Eye of the East," and the poets of Syria have styled it "the luster on the neck of doves," and historians said, "It is the golden clasp which couples the two sides of the world together." But if you come to Damascus to seek Aladdin's lamp and look for the genie that appeared if you rubbed the lamp's surface, as promised in *Arabian Nights*, you will be disappointed. Today Damascus presents a striking contrast between the old and the new. In the old town the streets are narrow and lined with miles of covered bazaars that are crowded with donkeys, carts, taxis, and pedestrians vying for space. It has always been a manufacturing city, and its various products overflow into the streets. Damasks, named after this city, are reversible fabrics—often made of silk—with elaborative patterns of animals, fruits, and landscapes woven into the fabric, and are a prominent commodity. Also famously available are specimens of damaskeening, by which steel and iron are graved and then the grooves filled with wire of gold.

But as absorbing as is the Damascus of today, I turn my

back on it—the bazaars boasting rugs with fabric of incomparable make; the baths that promise inspiration from ablution; and the shining brass, the crystal chandeliers; and the exquisite homes, marbled, divaned, fountained, upholstered, mosaicked, arabesqued, and colonnaded until nothing can be added. I turn my back on all these and see Damascus as it was when this narrow street, which the Bible calls "Straight," was a great, wide street, a New York Broadway or a Parisian Champs Elysees, a great thoroughfare crossing the city from gate to gate, along which tramped and rolled the pomp of all nations. There goes Abraham, the father of all the faithful. He has been in this city purchasing a celebrated slave. There goes Ben Hadad of Bible times, leading 32 conquered monarchs. There goes General Naaman, a man of patriotic pride—at least for the two rivers of his own country: the Abana (modern Barada, which flows through the city) and the Pharpar (present A'waj, providing water for the city). Naaman was disgruntled when the prophet Elisha told him to wash in the Jordan if he wanted to get rid of his leprosy. He cried out, "Are not Abana and Pharpar, the rivers of Damascus, better than all the waters of Israel? Couldn't I wash in them and be cleansed?" (2 Kings 5:12, NIV). There goes David—king, warrior, and sacred poet. There goes Tamerlane, the conqueror. There goes Haroun al Rashid, once the commander of an army of 99,000 Persians and Arabs. And more recently, in 1999, President Jimmy Carter meeting with Hafiz al Assad, the former president of Syria on the street called "Straight" at the west gate into the city.

I am awakened by a cry, a long drawn-out solo, compared to which a buzz saw is musical. It makes you inopportunely awake and will not let you sleep again. No longer does the muezzin appear high up in the different minarets and walk around the enclosed railing and cry in a sad and mumbling way, "God is great. I bear witness that there is no God but God. I bear witness that Muhammad is the apostle of God. Come to prayers! Come to salvation! God is great. There is no other but God. Prayers are better than sleep." The call to worship is prerecorded and sounds five times a day. I have seen the Muhammadan devotees in the Umayyad Mosque. As they begin, they turn toward the city of Mecca and then kneel on a rug that covers the entire floor of the mosque. With their thumbs touching the lobes of their ears, and holding their face between their hands, they cry, "God is great." Then folding their hands across their girdle, they look down and say, "Holiness to thee, O God, and praise be to thee. Great is thy name. Great is thy greatness. There is no deity but thee." Then the worshippers sit upon their heels, then touch their nose to the rug, and then their forehead, these genuflections are accompanied with the cry "Great is God." Then, raising the forefinger of their right hand toward heaven, they say, "I testify there is no deity but God, and I testify that Muhammad is the servant of God and the messenger of God." The prayer closes by the worshippers holding their hands opened upward as if to take the divine blessing, and then they rub their hands all over their face, as if to convey the blessing to their entire body.

One of the principal bazaars opens on this great mosque. Built in A.D. 635, it stands as the greatest monument to the Arab-Umayyad Empire. The mosque is reminiscent of the days when Damascus stood as the capital of the Muslim world, before the transfer of the capital to Baghdad.

The famous mosque is decorated with the finest mosaics of colored glass, gold, and mother of pearl. It was built where, about 1000 B.C., a pagan temple had stood and where later the Roman temple to Jupiter once stood. In the late fourth century A.D., Emperor Theodosius destroyed part of the temple and converted it into a church dedicated to John the Baptist, for tradition has it that here the head of the wilderness prophet is buried. A special chapel within the mosque stands over the cave in which John's head is said to be preserved in a golden casket.

The mosque is crowned with a tall minaret known by the Arabs as the "Minaret of Jesus." It is their belief that at His second coming Jesus will descend from heaven upon this minaret to judge the world and destroy the antichrist.

But what most stirs my soul is neither bazaar, nor mosque, nor palace, but a blind man passing along the street, small of stature and insignificant in personal appearance. Oh, yes, we have seen him before. He was one of that cavalcade coming from Jerusalem to Damascus to kill the Christians, and we saw him and his horse tumble up there on the road some distance from the city, and he got up blind. Yes, it is Saul of Tarsus now going along this street, called Straight. Instead of the proud Pharisee riding through the streets with the pomp of an inquisitor, we see a stricken man, trembling, groping, clinging to the hand of his guide. He is led into the house of Judas—not Judas the bad, but Judas the good.

In another part of the city one Ananias, not Ananias the liar, but Ananias the Christian, is told by the Lord to go to this house of Judas on Straight Street and to put his hand on the blind eyes of Saul so that his sight might return. Ananias feared that Saul might kill him. But the Lord said, "Go," and Ananias went.

There that violent persecutor sat in blindness. He was a great nature crushed. He had started for Damascus with the single purpose of assassinating Christ's followers, but since that confrontation with Jesus he was changed. Ananias stepped up to the sightless man, put his right thumb on one eye and the left thumb on the other eye, and, in an outburst of sympathy and love and faith, said, "Brother Saul, the Lord—Jesus, who appeared to you on the road as you were coming here—has sent me so that you may see again and be filled with the Holy Spirit" (Acts 9:17, NIV). Instantly something like scales fell from the blind man's eyes, and he arose from that seat the mightiest evangel of all the ages. He was a John Milton for sublimity of thought, a John Whitfield for popular eloquence, a Bill Gates for widespread philanthropy, but more than all of them put together, Paul was inspired, thunderbolted, multipotent, apostolic.

Did Judas, the kind host of this blind man, or Ananias, the visitor, see scales drop from the sightless eyes? I think not. But Paul knew they had fallen, and that is all that happens to any one of us when we are converted. The blinding scales drop from our eyes, and we see things differently. Anthony Robinson and Robert Wall describe conversion:

"Conversion, not conceived of in narrowly moral terms, is . . . seen as coming to a new understanding: it is having one's ignorance alleviated—changing one's mind as well as one's heart. Furthermore, conversion in Acts is almost always . . . connected to a call, to specific tasks, and to vocation. Conversion in Acts is less about pulling one's life together . . . than it is about being called and sent to do God's bidding."[1]

Speaking of Saul, the "penitent Pharisee," Ellen White wrote, "The inmost thoughts and emotions of his heart were transformed by divine grace; and his nobler faculties were brought into harmony with the eternal purposes of God."[2]

In the lexicon of religion, conversion is spoken of as "a personal experience," "being redeemed," "having a changed heart," "becoming a child of God," "accepting grace," "letting Jesus come into your heart," and "coming to know the Lord."

In the Old Testament, Ezekiel spoke of such religious conversion in terms of "a new heart and put a new spirit in you; I will remove from you your heart of stone and give you a heart of flesh" (Eze. 36:26, NIV). Jesus referred to the experience as being "born again," "repenting of sin," and "entering a narrow gate" (see John 3:3; Luke 24:47; Matt. 7:13, 14). The apostle Paul called it: "being alive from the dead," "transformed into a new creature," "a quickening," "regeneration" (see Rom. 6:13; Gal. 6:14, 15; 1 Cor. 15:44, 45; Titus 3:5). "Therefore, if anyone is in Christ, the new creation has come," Paul wrote, "the old has gone, the new is here!" (2 Cor. 5:17, NIV).

Joseph Alleine describes conversion as not "repairing of the old building" but rather taking it down and instead erecting "a new structure. The sincere Christian is quite a new fabric," he says, "from the foundation to the top-stone all new."[3] Persons outside religious faith rarely understand this terminology. Even many within the fold fail to comprehend the notion, for conversion has been an unexamined gift.

Some have sought to simplify it. We've all seen diagrams, charts, and four simple rules or spiritual laws to follow to conversion, as if converting a soul is like converting a sofa into a hide-a-bed. But describing a religious experience is something like describing a stunning sunset. It is a drama played out on the inner theater of the soul.

Perhaps it is best to learn about conversion by listening to those who have experienced it, as the way the church used to do in "testimony meetings." While religious experiences can be suffocatingly subjective, and hearing about some people's conversions is like hearing about their operation, it remains the most effective way to learn about what transpires in that phenomenon known as a religious experience.

Besides the startling and dramatic conversion of Saul recorded in Acts 9:3-9, briefly, here are four famous conversion experiences. Listen to them from the standpoint of whether or not you have experienced anything similar.

The first conversion experience is that of Martin Luther, described by Roland Bainton: "On a sultry day in July of the year 1505, a lonely traveler was trudging over a parched road on the outskirts of the Saxon village of Stotterheim. . . . As he approached the village, the sky became overcast. Suddenly, there was a shower, then a crashing storm. A bolt of lightning that rived the gloom and knocked the man to the ground. Struggling to rise, he cried in terror, "St. Anne help me! I will become a monk."[4]

Yet another famous conversion is that of John Wesley, founder of the Methodist Church. He wrote: "In the evening I went very unwillingly to a society in Aldersgate Street. Some unnamed person was reading from Martin Luther's notes on Paul's Epistle to the Romans when, about a quarter of nine, while he was describing the change which God works in the heart through faith in Christ, I felt my heart strangely warmed."[5]

The next conversion we will relate is that of Billy Sunday, the fiery demonstrable Chicago Cub baseball player who became a popular evangelist. He testified: "I rose from my knees, and all my feelings seemed to rise and flow out; and the utterance of my heart was, 'I want to pour my whole soul out to God.' Deep happiness came over me; I felt I was accepted into the inner circle of God's loved ones. I walked out of that mission and couldn't help praising the Lord. As I went along the street, I lifted up one foot, and it seemed to say 'Glory!' and I lifted up the other, and it seemed to say 'Amen,' and they kept up like that all the time I was walking."[6]

"Salvation," he wrote, "to some is just as big a change as crawling out of a snow bank and going into a warm room."[7]

The final conversion is of an English poet and hymn writer William Cowper, who in 1763 was committed to the private asylum of Dr. Nathaniel Cotton in St. Albans. For eight months he endured the tortures of a mind diseased. A dreadful melancholia settled over his soul. He could see nothing but the lowering clouds of misery and hopelessness of his wretchedness. Nothing seemed to lift his spirits; the future was blank, black, void, meaningless. On occasion he would take up his Bible to find hope and comfort, only to fling it from him as the demons of despair wrestled for his mind.

Then came a certain morning when, feeling somewhat more cheerful and chipper, he stumbled upon the therapy of Romans 3. Here is Cowper's own account of it: "The happy period which was to shake off my fetters, and afford me a clear opening of the free mercy of God in Christ Jesus, was now arrived. I flung myself into a chair near the window, and, seeing a Bible there, ventured once more to apply to it for comfort and instruction. The first verse I saw was the twenty-fifth [verse] of the third [chapter] of Romans: 'Whom God hath set forth to be a propitiation through faith in his blood, to declare his righteousness for the remission of sins that are past, through the fornearance of God.' Immediately I received strength to believe it, and the full beams of the Sun of Righteousness shone upon me. I saw the sufficiency of the atonement He had made, my pardon in His blood, and all the fullness and completeness of His justification. In a moment, I believed and received the gospel."[8]

What a change was wrought in Cowper's life by the marvelous balm of this text in the book of Romans. I will not tell you that from that moment on he became the soul of good cheer and the personification of spontaneous lightheartedness. On the contrary, he still suffered from bouts of depression and gloom.

The apostle Paul addressed this reality when he wrote of Christians taking "off [the] old self, with its practices" and putting "on the new self, which is being renewed in knowledge in the image of its Creator" (Col. 3:9, NIV). Does Paul identify the new person with sinless perfection? The phrase "being renewed" signifies that the new person is not yet perfect. One could say that we are now *genuinely* new, though not yet *totally* new. But new we are—and so we ought to see ourselves.

To be sure, we still sin daily, and as in Cowper's situation, he was still afflicted with anxieties. But when we do, we do not revert to the "old self" state any more than we suddenly become unregenerate. When we who are adults do childish things, we don't suddenly become children; we remain adults who, for the moment, are not acting like adults. The fact that believers remain new persons in Christ should be a constant incentive for us to reflect that newness in new ways of thinking, talking, and living. This is why Cowper was always able to rise above his miseries and triumph over his troubles. He was able to go on his way rejoicing in his newfound hope.

William Cowper, the hopeless, helpless creature of the asylum, responded to the most thrilling therapy in all God's universe; and his heart overflowed with such a singing gladness that he still enriches our hymn books, though he has been dead for almost two centuries. Here is his own powerful testimony:

"I was a stricken deer, that left the herd
Long since; with many an arrow deep infixt
My panting side was charg'd, when I withdrew
To seek a tranquil death in distant shades.
There was I found by one, who had himself
Been hurt by th' archers. In his side he bore,
And in his hands and feet, the cruel scars.
With gentle force soliciting the darts,
He drew them forth, and heal'd, and bade me live."[9]

And may I point out that the "One who had Himself been hurt by the archers" still has His ancient power to calm the troubled breast and bring peace to the anguished. Jesus specializes in miracles of grace for those who, like the unhappy Cowper and the wretched, blind Paul, feel the weight of guilt and remorse in their souls and who have no hope but death. He can enter the feelings of our infirmities because He has experienced the weight of the sins of the world pressing down upon His own soul. Thus He can draw the vicious darts and arrows that pierce the soul, and bid you live. Cowper's asylum was transformed into the gate of heaven.

Those are the conversion experiences of five different individuals, spanning more than 2,000 years. Some had the flash and noise of lightning and thunder, and others the subdued warmth and quiet of a "heartwarming experience." All five were life-changing experiences. Paul had been a persecutor; Luther, a rebellious man; Wesley, a lackadaisical preacher; Billy Sunday was fast becoming a skid-row bum; and William Cowper, a wretched melancholic. Much good came from those five conversions. Certainly, in the words of the eighteenth-century statesman George Lyttelton, "the conversion and apostleship of St. Paul alone . . . was of itself a demonstration sufficient to prove Christianity to be a divine revelation."[10]

Millions of lesser-knowns have testified to similar conversion experiences. A government worker in Washington, D.C., says, "I had the feeling that a hand had been laid on my shoulder and turned me around in a complete about-face." A former Miss America reflected, "There was a wrenching and tearing, and then there was a flood of warmth that was overpowering . . . so very much happiness filled me that I did not feel I could contain it all." An English author writes, "When the Holy Spirit entered my heart, He heightened every aspect of life, like a sixth sense." A college student in New York says, "I can never forget the indescribable ecstasy of the moment." So for some, conversion is a painful experience; for others, pure joy. For some it is explosive; others find it quiet and gradual. It is intellectual, it is emotional, it is volitional. Conversion seems patterned to the personality, but for all, in whatever form, it is the supreme moral moment.

A poet wrote, "For it is one thing to see the land of peace from a wooded ridge . . . and another to tread the road that leads to it." Many people do not make the journey. Those who do, like Paul, know the reality of scales falling from their eyes. The diary of the former United Nations secretary-general Dag Hammarskjold has the following entry for a day in 1961: "At some moment I did answer yes to Someone—or Something—and from that hour I was certain that existence is meaningful and that therefore my life, in self-surrender, had a goal."

So, as Robinson and Wall submit, "'conversion' means crossing boundaries and barriers and reaching a whole new way of seeing and understanding life" as did Ananias, who "was converted for the purpose of ministering to Saul/Paul." Robinson and Wall are right in saying that "Ananias was understandably reluctant to put himself in the presence of the one who had so recently been putting Christians in chains, in prison, and on trial." They add, "What a moment it must have been when Saul, able to see again, saw the Christian Ananias standing before him as God's instrument of healing! Portraits of conversion in Acts are many and varied."[11]

The goal of conversion is to have the scales removed from our eyes by the touch of Ananias. Conversion leads you to see all subjects and all things differently—God, Christ, and eternity. "When the mind of man is brought into communion with the mind of God, the finite with the Infinite," writes Ellen White, "the effect on body, and mind, and soul, is beyond estimate."[12] Indeed, great is the soul's joyful surprise when the scales fall from the eyes and the long spiritual darkness is ended, when we look up into the Father's face, always radiant and loving, but now for the first time revealed, when our blindness is forever gone and we cry, "Thank God!" But is conversion its own end, or is there more? Shall not our visit to Damascus result like Paul's visit, in vision to the blind and increased vision for those who saw somewhat before? I say to you as Ananias did to Saul of Tarsus when his sympathetic fingers touched the closed eyelids, "Brother Saul, the Lord—Jesus, who appeared to you on the road as you were coming here—has sent me so that you may see again and be filled with the Holy Spirit."

---

[1] Anthony B. Robinson and Robert W. Wall, *Called to Be Church: The Book of Acts for a New Day* (Grand Rapids: Eerdmans, 2006), p. 141. "It would be difficult," writes Mikeal C. Parsons, "to overestimate the significance of the conversion and call of Paul for the narrative of Acts, or indeed, for the course of early Christian history. But there is debate as to whether the event was a 'conversion' or a 'call.'" But Parsons concludes that "Paul's Damascus Road experience . . . is presented as both a conversion *and* a call, both in his letters . . . and in Acts. . . . By the end of the episode the zealous persecutor of Christ and his church has been radically transformed and has become the zealous missionary persecuted in Christ's name and for his church" (*Acts* [Grand Rapids: Baker Academic, 2008], p. 135).

[2] Ellen G. White, *The Acts of the Apostles* (Mountain View, Calif.: Pacific Press Pub. Assn., 1911), p. 120.

[3] *The Encyclopedia of Religious Quotations,* ed. Frank S. Mead (New York: Fleming H. Revell, 1965), s.v. "Conversion."

[4] Roland H. Bainton, *Here I Stand: A Life of Martin Luther* (New York: Abingdon Press, 1950), p. 21.

[5] *A Treasury of Great Preaching,* ed. Clyde E. Fant, Jr., and William M. Pinson, Jr. (Dallas: Word Publishing, 1995), pp. 5, 6.

[6] William A. "Billy" Sunday, *The Sawdust Trail: Billy Sunday in His Own Words* (Iowa City: University of Iowa Press, 2005), p. 50. "Sunday's conver-

sion was not without its effect. He gave up drinking, swearing, gambling, and giving up theaters, and he refused to play baseball on Sunday" (p. 7).

[7] William G. McLoughlin, Jr., *Billy Sunday Was His Real Name* (Chicago: Chicago University Press, 1955), p. 129.

[8] William Cowper, *Memoir of the Early Life of William Cowper, Esq.* (London: R. Edwards, 1816), p.67.

[9] John Piper, *The Hidden Smile of God* (Wheaton, Il: Crossway Books, 2001), p. 100.

[10] Quoted in F. F. Bruce, *The Book of Acts*, p. 196.

[11] Robinson and Wall, p. 141.

[12] E G. White, *The Acts of the Apostles*, p. 126.

2 ANTIOCH:
CONTROVERSY TO CONCILIATION

"Now Paul and his company . . . came to Antioch in Pisidia"
(Acts 13:13, 14).

Phillips Brooks, in a most stimulating sermon entitled "Symbol and Reality," argues, "There is no better test of man's progress than this advancing power to do without the things which used to be essential to their lives." He then uses the illustration of climbing a mountain to explain the need for the climber to "let the lower foothold go" once he or she has secured the next-higher foothold. "The lives of men who have been always growing," says Brooks, "are strewed along their whole course with the things which they have learned to do without." What an overburdened life ours would be if we were compelled to carry all the old things we once valued and used with us as we advanced to the new!

The early disciples appropriately refused the burden of Mosaic symbols and forms, which had had their day, done their work, and ceased to be. But the pet ideas and practices that have long absorbed the unwarranted interest of many do not die without a struggle. Some champions linger on and show fight at every opportunity.

The Judaizing party in Jerusalem made desperate attempts to resist Christianity. First, there was a blind and indiscriminate attachment to old opinions. They had been brought up in the belief that the Mosaic institutions were unchangeable. The very suggestion of a modification of them was considered treason against Moses and against God. They had been brought up to believe that they, exclusively, were the people of God. Their proud and selfish hearts rebelled against the idea that others could have equal access to their arrogantly guarded privileges. They had cherished a contempt and hatred for all other nations; how could Christians believe that those nations were as much objects of the love of God as they themselves were? They had fattened in their opinion and self-perception that they were morally superior to others. They refused to accept a gospel that taught them that they could be justified only by grace, and that they must seek that grace on a par with all other sinners, through the merits of Jesus Christ. They would admit a Christianity that left the Law of Moses intact and obliged all Christians to become Jews, so to speak; that exalted their nation and left the prejudices of their childhood undisturbed. These Judaizers "came down from Judea to Antioch" (Acts 15:1, NIV).

Antioch was the chief and military center of southern Galatia. It was Phrygian in language and tradition; hence one inscription speaks of the "Phrygian" Antioch. Jews were encouraged to settle at Antioch, which was a cosmopolitan city with a culture that evoked the admiration of Cicero himself. Pompey captured the city in 64 B.C. Emperor Augustus made it a Roman colony, giving it the title Colonia Caesarea, and it became the third-largest city of the Roman Empire. It boasted magnificent buildings and temples and lamp-lit streets, earning the epithets "Antioch the Beautiful" and "The Queen of the East."

Charles F. Pfeiffer's *The Biblical World* states, "Religiously, Antioch was a mixture of the best and the worst. The groves of Daphne and the Apollo sanctuary were scenes of orgiastic rites." The book then cites a poem by the Roman satirist Juvenal (c. A.D. 60–140) that uses the river Orontes as a metaphor "of the corruption which was entering Rome to the East."[1]

However, Christians in Antioch were able to preach freely to both Jew and Gentile, and it was from the church in Antioch that the first foreign missionaries went forth as heralds of the cross. There was a Jewish colony in this city and, therefore, a synagogue. On the first Sabbath day following their arrival in this city, Paul and Barnabas came here and took their places among the congregation. At the invitation of the ruler of the synagogue, Paul was invited to deliver the address.

It was in Antioch that the followers of Jesus were first called "Christians." It was in Antioch that Paul first said to the Christian community, "Even if you had ten thousand guardians in Christ, you do not have many fathers, for in Christ Jesus I became your father through the gospel. Therefore I urge you to imitate me. . . . What do you prefer? Shall I come to you with a rod of discipline, or shall I come in love with a gentle spirit?" (1 Cor. 4:15-21, NIV).

Paul's first quarrel with the community came as a result of his insistence that Gentile converts need not become Jews to accept Christ. The Jewish Christians, vastly in the majority, were vocally outraged, and in the presence of Gentiles who were drawn to them, Paul said, "I wish those who unsettle you would mutilate themselves!" (Gal. 5:12, RSV). He was not less sarcastic to those Christians who insisted that to be a true follower of Jesus one must live as meekly and as inoffensively as a slave, for, as he later often and furiously repeated, "you gladly put up with fools since you are so wise! In fact, you even put up with anyone who enslaves you or exploits you or takes advantage of you or puts on airs or slaps you in the face. To my shame I admit that we were too weak for that!" (2 Cor. 11:19-21, NIV).

To Paul, many of the Christians of Antioch were even more exasperating than some of the Nazarenes in Jerusalem. Additionally, the elders of the church were offended by how tersely and swiftly he disposed of their dissensions and intense scrupulousness. Young though the church was, it was already beset by a multitude of interpreters who asserted that they had received divine inspiration and that their opinions must be accepted.

Among these self-professed interpreters were the Judaizers who came up to Antioch and, with volunteered assiduity, created dissension. These Jewish teachers seem, on this occasion, to have acted not in open antagonism to Paul but rather of clandestine intrigue. They came as "spies" into an enemy's camp, creeping in unawares and gradually insinuating or openly inculcating their opinion that circumcision and submission to the Mosaic Law were necessary to salvation. Further, these Judean visitors refused all social interaction with uncircumcised persons, and that included the common participation in the Lord's Supper (see Acts 15:5). Thus the two controversial issues of the way of salvation and fellowship between Jewish and Gentile Christians were introduced into the Antiochene church.

But the trouble was not confined to Antioch; it spread to the young churches of southern Galatia. Judaizers visited these churches and urged that Christians were obligated to observe circumcision and Jewish ceremonial law as an essential part of their faith in Jesus. With white-hot urgency Paul wrote his Epistle to the Galatians in order to combat these errors, not with abuse, but argument. Though he was tender and considerate toward his opponents (see Gal. 4:19), we have to mark his unflinching firmness and boldness.

To complicate matters further, Peter was in residence at Antioch when the Judean emissaries arrived. At first Peter ate freely with Gentile Christians; his experience on the roof of Simon's house at Joppa and in the house of Cornelius at

Caesarea had taught him not to "call any man common or unclean" (Acts 10:28, NKJV). But when the Judeans arrived and expressed their viewpoint so dogmatically, he withdrew from Gentile society and sat at the table with circumcised persons only. His actions endangered not only the principle of Christian unity but also the fundamental gospel principle that salvation was the gift of God's grace in Christ, to be received by faith alone. For this reason Paul "opposed him [Peter] to his face" (Gal. 2:11, NIV).

Saul's encounters with Simon Peter had not been the happiest. Simon Peter, a brawny fisherman, was not of Saul's subtle and colorful mind. He was as stubborn as Saul and frequently as obdurate, and often their voices rose to acrimonious heights.

Had Saul seen the Messiah in the flesh? Had he walked with Him in the dust? Had he witnessed His crucifixion? Had the Messiah imparted to him wondrous things over many days? Saul claimed to have seen the Messiah in the desert, and Peter did not doubt this for an instant. But first he had persecuted the followers of the Messiah as no Roman would. Who had slept next to the Messiah and broken bread with Him but Simon Peter? Had Peter not walked with Him for 40 days after He had risen from the tomb? Yes, this Saul of Tarshish, this Pharisee, this man of Greek and Roman knowledge and worldly ways, this man of haughty intellect, appeared to believe that he understood the Messiah better than did those who had dwelt with Him! It was very vexatious.

Some would argue that heresies, that is, divisions and separations of opinion, are necessary in order for truth and that which is commendable to be made manifest. Conflict sifts the chaff of falsehood from the genuine wheat of truth. But it is not enough to indulge in continuing "dissension and debate"; the issues must be discussed and decided "at the highest level."

Thus it was that a general conference convened in Jerusalem. But why Jerusalem?

Christianity started out in Jerusalem. The disciples fulfilled their Lord's command and "began at Jerusalem." The gospel was first preached at Jerusalem. The Holy Ghost endowed the Christian teachers and sealed the Christian believers first at Jerusalem. The church first took form at Jerusalem. Its officers were first appointed at Jerusalem. The constitution of the Jerusalem church cannot be known for certain, but it is clear that Peter had no exclusive authority, and that if disputes and controversies were submitted to an apostolic council, their decision took the form of recommendation and not of command.

So to Jerusalem came Paul and Barnabas as the delegates of the Antiochene church. They brought to the members of the church at Jerusalem an account of all "that God had done with them," but more to deliberate with the responsible leaders. It required no small heroism to go into the very stronghold of Judaism and there, before James, Peter, the Pharisees, and the most Judaizing members of the churches of Judea, proclaim the gospel of the grace of God (Gal. 2:2; Acts 15:12) and the free admission of the Gentiles into Christ's church.

The stage was set. The position of Judaizers was reactionary. It aimed to reestablish circumcision as a condition of salvation. This was going from the "spirit" back to the "flesh," from the position of the internal to that of an external religion. It was substituting works for faith, doing for being, as the condition of salvation. The Juidaizers put forth their claims sharply. Now the whole question was open, and the air was full of debate.

The Jews seemed to have the vantage ground. Circumcision was unquestionably a divine institution, and the Christians could not prove that it had been formally removed. It formed a good ground on which to fight. The Christian teachers could urge only that the "life in Christ" no longer needed formal bonds and that God's grace in Christ was given to those who were not circumcised. Paul took very firm ground on the question in dealing with those who felt the helpfulness of rites and ceremonies. He resisted any tampering with the gospel condition of salvation by way of formal ordinance or ceremony.

On the one hand, the Jews understood humanity's reconciliation with God as a covenant relation that had to be sacrificially and ceremonially maintained. On the other hand, Christianity presented Jesus' all-sufficient sacrifice for sin and authority to forgive—to be accepted in faith and penitence—as the basis for humanity's reconciliation with God. The two systems are related as a shadow is related to the figure that throws it, but the two cannot be *combined*; the shadow must pass altogether when the substance has come. The salvation humanity wants is a soul salvation, and that no rite, no ceremonial, can touch.

At first, salvation was, in effect, a divine favor granted to one particular race. Later, outsiders were admitted to share the "salvation," or "standing with God," of the Abrahamic race by submitting to the rite of circumcision. As spirituality faded from the Jewish life, people attached increasing importance to the mere rite, and zealous groups contended for these observances as if the hope of salvation lay in them alone. Ritual has an important place and role, but giving it a different, unwarranted role is ever perilous to spiritual truth. "It is a useful handmaid; it is a tyrannous mistress."[2]

Not works of righteousness, but "faith," which presupposes penitence, was Paul's position. How are sinners saved? Apart from all systems or ceremonies, they must accept the salvation God freely offers them in the person of His Son, Jesus Christ. The act of acceptance is called "faith." Paul's attitude in coming to the counsel had its replication many years later when the electoral prince of Brandenburg said to his envoy as he proceeded to a conference with the papists: "Bring me the little word *sola* [i.e., *alone*, faith *only*] back—or come not back at all!"[3]

Four leading speeches and arguments are recorded. Peter's is first (see Acts 15:9-11). He had recovered from his capitulation in Antioch and openly sided with Paul. First, he appealed to his experience at Caesarea. It is clear that the Gentiles, no less than Jewish Christians, had received the Holy Ghost. Surely this was significant proof that God had already decided the debate. God, Paul had already learned, was "no respecter of persons" (Acts 10:34). In other words, God has made no difference between them; has placed them upon the one footing. Second, Paul appealed to history by reminding them what a heavy yoke the Jewish law had proved to be for many generations; how thankful they were to be relieved from the legal bondage by the salvation offered through faith, and how unreasonable it would be to attempt to impose on others a burden that neither they nor their fathers had ever been able to bear.

Then followed Barnabas and Paul with their missionary tidings. These carried volumes of conviction. Isn't it true that we still listen wonderfully to preached sermons and facts and reliable testimony? With what keenness of attention and almost sympathetic pride they listened to these recitals from the lips of men who had "hazarded their lives for the name of [their] Lord Jesus Christ" (Acts 15:26).

After these thrilling speeches James (probably "the brother of the Lord" and writer of the general epistle by the same name) renewed the argument, corroborating it by Old Testament scripture quotation. He laid down "calling on the Name of God" as the condition for incorporation into the kingdom of God. The heathen people who were converted had already fulfilled this condition. Further, it is the Lord "who doeth all these things" (verse 17). It was James's decision that he would not have the Gentile Christians, who were turning in repentance and good works to God, harassed. He would recognize their evangelical freedom, would reject the demands of the Judaizing party; in fact, he fully, though on different grounds, coincided with Paul. At the same time, he insisted on certain moral and ceremonial abstinences. According to Eusebius, when the debate was over, James knelt unceasingly in the Temple, praying for the forgiveness of his people.

But note, James did not sit down after the council without making definite proposals. There was unanimous agreement that the apostles and elders would write and send what they wrote by the honored hands of Paul, Barnabas, and two others specially delegated from their own home communion to Antioch. In this way, the churches were assured that the emissaries were delivering, not their own private opinion, but the deliberate judgment of the church. The words of the letter called for kindly respect, conciliatory tone toward all, fidelity of truth, "honor to whom honor" is due, religious calling to witness of the Ruler of the Church, "the Holy Ghost" (verses 23-29).

The four peacemakers sped on their way to Antioch. They called "the multitude" together, delivered their letter, and congratulated the Gentiles liberated from many a fear in its "consolation." The two visitors, Judas and Silas, also addressed the church in Antioch, the latter of whom remained in Antioch to assist Paul and Barnabas in their ministry.

What can we learn from the problem-solving strategy James employed?

Consultation: We learn that we must take a stance of humble, reasonable, and redemptive consultation rather than condescension when we engage with those whose opinions and convictions differ from ours. Where could you find two good men who have taken more divergent views of the gospel of Christ than did James and Paul? Had they come to this council intent on magnifying their own distinctive points, bitter conflict and fatal rupture would have ensued. But they strove to meet one another, and their encounter resulted in peace and the furtherance of redeeming truth. "While looking to God for divine guidance," writes Ellen White, "he [Paul] was ever ready to recognize the authority vested in the body of believers. . . . He felt the need of counsel; and when the need arose, he was glad to lay these before the church and unite with his brethren in seeking God for wisdom to make right decisions."[4]

Accommodation: We deduce that individuals of divergent thought should strive to meet one another's views. The church at Antioch was not obliged to consult that at Jerusalem; the latter having no jurisdiction entitling it to decide disputes of the former. Often when no written constitution obliges us to refer to authorities, it is a matter of practical wisdom, and therefore of rectitude, to go outside our own "body" and submit our case to those of high repute. We may gain far more than we thereby lose. Accommodating is a win-win step.

Concession: We conclude that equitable compromise may be the most honorable settlement. The Jewish party conceded to the Gentile party by waiving the requirement for Gentile circumcision; the Gentile party conceded to the Jewish party by agreeing to observe certain statutes. Frequently, occasions will occur when each side owes it to the other to make a concession. The spirit that strives for victory is not the spirit of Christ. It is an honor and a joy to concede—when we can conscientiously do so—to Christian brethren who differ from us.

Completion: We recognize that decisions, once attained, should be courteously and carefully carried out (see verses

22, 33). The church at Jerusalem, though it had yielded to the church at Antioch, did not give way sulkily or grudgingly. It did not dismiss the deputation with a cold and formal resolution. It sent able and influential men, with letters, to accompany Paul and Barnabas, and these greeted the Syrian church and laid the matter fully before them. And in the end, the two communities understood each other and rejoiced. What is done in Christ's name and cause should be done with utmost courtesy and with perfect thoroughness.

Submission: We understand that we may rest happy in the all-seeing wisdom and all-embracing love of God (see verses 14-18). James intimated that what was then happening was only the fulfillment of the divine intention. "God's purpose," writes Ellen White, was "to bestow upon the Gentiles the same privileges and blessings that had been granted to the Jews."[5]

Finally, the decision-making process included the Holy Spirit. "It seemed best to the Holy Spirit and to us" (verse 15:28). Citing various examples throughout Acts wherein the apostles directly acknowledge, invoke, or represent the Holy Spirit's involvement, Parsons comments that "the addition of the Holy Spirit adds authoritative weight to the church's decision."[6]

When we are baffled by perplexities, we need to remember that all things are in the hands of the Omniscient One. When distressed by the disappointments and difficulties of our work, let us be consoled by remembering that God means to restore humankind; His love and wisdom will prevail, though we may not see the way and though our fears abound.

Thus, James, with this fivefold strategy, gave voice to the decision of the church.

Following the council in Jerusalem, the church in Antioch prospered. Paul knew that he must leave the church there, for the sandy soil had been replaced by rock; leaders were ordained, and converts, sought with love, responded. Truly, in much less than 20 years since the Crucifixion, the harvest as well as the laborers had increased, and the gospel had spread even to Rome and Athens, to quiet, little colonies, and to Egypt and other lands. It insistently crept like a small, unassuming plant filled with purple blossoms, and it covered the aridity of the soil of people's lives. It made their arduous duties fragrant and their pain, slavery, and taxes under Rome more bearable.

We end where we began. The gospel frees us from all burdensome imposts (Acts 15:10). Why tempt God by putting an intolerable yoke on the disciples' necks? Why invite defeat? Why multiply difficulty and ensure disappointment by requiring of the whole Gentile world a conformity that they will not render and that God does not demand? Why make burdensome the yoke that the Master Himself made easy? (See Matt. 11:30.) The gospel of grace was meant to be a source of blessedness and deliverance; would it not be insensate and foolish to tie it to institutes that would turn it into an insufferable vexation? As Brooks reminds us, these are things we can do without!

---

[1] Charles F. Pfeiffer, ed., *The Biblical World* (Grand Rapids: Baker Book House, 1972), s.v. "Antioch (Syrian)."

[2] R. Tuck, in *The Pulpit Commentary: Acts of the Apostles*, ed. H.D.M. Spence and Joseph S. Exell (London: Funk and Wagnalls, n.d.), vol. 42, p. 21.

[3] E. Johnson, in *The Pulpit Commentary: Acts of the Apostles*, vol. 42, pp. 13, 14.

[4] E. G. White, *The Acts of the Apostles,* p. 200.

[5] *Ibid.*, p. 194.

[6] M. C. Parsons, *Acts*, pp. 216, 217.

3 PHILIPPI:
SUICIDE TO SALVATION

"Sirs, what must I do to be saved?" (Acts 16:30, NIV).

I am standing in the Philippian dungeon. I can feel the chill. I can hear the groan of the incarcerated ones who have not seen the sunlight for years; the deep sigh of women who remember their father's house and mourn over their wasted estates; the cough of a consumptive; the struggle of one in a horrific nightmare; a culprit, his chains rattling as he rolls over in his dreams. But, there is another sound. It is a song of joy and gladness! The music comes winding through the corridors of the prison, and in all the dark wards the whisper is heard: "What is that?" "What is that?" It is the song of two men. The long gashes on their backs, still oozing blood, are grisly evidence of an ugly whipping. They lie flat on the cold ground, their feet fast in wooden sockets. They cannot sleep, but they can sing. "Jailer, what are you doing with these people? Why have they been put here?" "Oh, they have been trying to make the world better." "Is that all?" "That is all." A pit for Joseph. A lions' cave for Daniel. A blazing furnace for Shadrach. And a dungeon for Paul and Silas.

Paul was on his second missionary journey. Accompanied by Silas, Luke, and Timothy, he was directed in a vision to the western shore of the Aegean, and he planted the faith in Philippi, Thessalonica, and Corinth before he settled in Ephesus.

He sailed from Troas to the north Aegean, arriving in Neapolis, the port of Philippi on the Macedonian coast. Philippi was located on the Egnatian Way, 10 miles inland from the Aegean. This city received its name from Philip II of Macedon. In 350 B.C. Alexander passed through Philippi on his trip from Amphipolis to Thrace. The city entered history again in 42 B.C. when Antony and Octavian defeated Brutus and Cassius (the assassins of Julius Caesar) west of the city. After the battle of Philippi, Antony ordered Roman soldiers to settle in Philippi, which became a Roman colony. Octavian settled other colonists there after his victory over Antony and Cleopatra at Actium in 31 B.C. The city, as a result, had a mixed population: the original Thracians, Greeks, and Romans.

When Paul visited a new city, he usually attended the local Jewish synagogue on the first Sabbath after his arrival in order to make the Christian message known "to the Jew first." At Philippi, however, there was no synagogue. But there was an unofficial meeting place outside the city where a number of women came together. Paul and his companions found this place, by the banks of the river Gangites, and sat down with the women and told them the story of Jesus.

One of these women, a God-fearing Gentile from Thyatira in the province of Asia, was Lydia. She had come to Philippi as a trader of purple dye. "The Lord opened her heart to give heed to what was said by Paul" (Acts 16:14, RSV), and she became Paul's first convert in Europe and was baptized with her household.

On the other hand, another, quite different convert of Paul's—a "pythoness," as Luke described her—was regarded as inspired by Apollo to give oracles. People accepted her involuntary utterances as the voice of God, and she was highly sought after by people who wished to have their fortunes told. She followed the missionaries through the streets of Philippi, advertising them aloud as servants of the Most High God. Paul, vexed by her continual clamor, cast out the spirit that possessed her. But though Paul's deed was good, the fortunetelling slave girl's owners did not appreciate it in the least. In exorcizing the evil spirit, he had exorcized their source of income as well. They perceived Paul's act as an attack on their sacred property rights, and so they dragged Paul and Silas before the magistrates. After all, these vagabond Jews were causing disturbances in the city and teaching customs that Roman citizens, of all people, could never admit or practice. Because of the laws that were in place prohibiting foreign religious propaganda among Roman citizens, the magistrates had the missionaries stripped, soundly beaten, and locked up in jail.[1]

While I am standing in the gloom of that Philippian dungeon and hear the mingling of voices, sobs, groans, and both blasphemy and hallelujah, suddenly, an earthquake! The iron bars of the prison twist, the pillars crack like sticks, the solid masonry begins to heave and rock till all the doors swing open, and the walls fall with a terrible crash. The jailer, feeling himself responsible for these prisoners and feeling suicide to be honorable (since Socrates, Cato, and Cassius killed themselves), put his sword to his own heart, proposing with one strong, keen thrust to put an end to his agitation. But Paul cries out, "Don't harm yourself! We are all here!" Then I see the jailer running through the dust, dodging the debris, throwing himself at the feet of the prisoners, and crying out: "What shall I do?" Did Paul say, "Get out of this place before the aftershock; put handcuffs and hopples on these other prisoners, lest they get away"? No such word! Instead, a compact, thrilling, tremendous answer, an answer memorable through the centuries: "Believe on the Lord Jesus Christ, and thou shalt be saved" (Acts 16:31).

When the jailer said, "I believe," he was embarking on a spiritual pilgrimage. The trip is one of adventure and excitement. It is also one fraught with many pitfalls, a journey full of surprises. But this belief is not nonrational, something that has to do only with the heart and not at all with the mind. Tertullian early propounded the idea that believing something because it is absurd is a noble thing to do. Actually, he is not far from many contemporary thinkers who call us to a kind of blind faith in the midst of meaninglessness. This may be courageous, but it is this kind of "faith" that is far removed from the New Testament concept.

The New Testament does not call us to crucify our intellect. A call to faith in the New Testament is not an invitation to embrace contradictions and irrationality. The New Testament does not elevate irrationality and incoherence as religious values. Faith is reasonable. That is not to say that faith is to be confused with rationalism, which gives a much too one-sided emphasis on the mind's ability to understand all reality unaided. Nor is faith so one sided that it obscures noncognitive elements in it. Truth is always involved with the mind. But if truth will touch my life at some point, I must have understanding.

In biblical terms, there is an inescapable relationship between my *act* of believing and the *content* of what it is I believe. As soon as the believer says they believe, they go on to say what it is they believe. Thus, the jailer was not called to a faith in general but to faith in particular—namely, to faith in a person and in the work of Jesus Christ.

There are three vital aspects of faith: intellectual content, mental assent, and personal trust.

Faith as intellectual content. Faith as intellectual content has to do with the revelation communicated in the Bible. It includes a belief that God exists, that He has entered the world by incarnation in the person of Jesus Christ, and that in Christ our redemption is secured through His life, death, resurrection, and ascension. Is it possible for someone to hear and understand the message and not agree that the message is true? Yes, but to be aware of its content and to disclaim its truth is to be in a state of unbelief. True faith involves more.

Faith as mental assent. A person must not only know that Christ died upon the cross but also believe that His death was an atoning act. But does the acceptance of the content of the message constitute saving faith? According to the Scriptures, it is possible for one to have a perfect grasp of theology and still be barred from the kingdom. The pen of the apostle James almost drips with sarcasm as he clearly indicates that faith involves far more than mental assent (see James 2:19, 20). Even demons assent to the facts of faith, but they do not possess faith in the *saving* sense of the word. True faith does have a mental dimension, but it does not stand alone. It involves more.

Faith as personal trust. We may describe a personal, trusting faith as the heart's disposition toward Christ. Conversely, those without true faith remain indifferent, aloof, or hostile toward God. A person may have a mental dimension of faith and still be outside a living, loving relationship with God that is possible only through faith. True faith involves more than being persuaded that something is true. It involves loving the truth. It means more than assenting to Christ; it means delighting in Him.

But, true faith is not divorced from the realities of life. Preachers are not to offer congregations a fantasy world of theological myths into which they can escape from their daily problems. When people discover unexpectedly that they must experience the full reality of, say, tragic disease and go through the valley of the shadow of death in spite of their faith, their faith is shattered. If we think that God has promised us a life of prosperity free from sickness and free from tragedy and then suddenly encounter one of those problems, we are inclined to have a crisis of faith, even think God has abandoned us. Away with phony promises of superficial grace! Such faith may talk much of Jesus Christ, but it presents Him as a Dale Carnegie in robe and sandals. The Bible indicates that Christians in this world must suffer many things, but even in the midst of these difficulties, He has promised us His presence. Ellen G. White says, "Trials will come; but go forward. . . . Faith lightens every burden, relieves every weariness. Providences that are now mysterious you may solve by continued trust in God."[2]

Martin Luther King wrote of a time he was worn out by endless worry. Then he received, by letter and telephone, a mounting series of threats to him and to his family. He knew they were serious. One night, after an especially exhausting day, he had gone to bed when the phone rang, and an angry voice promised violence soon. King got out of bed and paced back and forth, he brewed coffee, and with his courage almost gone, he wondered how to quit. Then at the kitchen table he bowed his head on his hands and told God, "I am at the end of my powers, I have nothing left. I've come to the point where I can't face it alone." Then, "at that moment," he says, "I experienced the presence of the Divine as I had never before experienced God. It seemed as though I could hear the quiet assurance of an inner voice. . . . Almost at once my fears began to pass from me. . . . God had given me an inner calm."[3] We as preachers do not offer "cleverly devised myths" when we talk about the divine reinforcement. "He restoreth my soul" is literally true. "When in faith we take hold of His strength, He will change, wonderfully change, the most hopeless, discouraging outlook."[4]

There is no human accounting for the way people of faith

react from blows that should be crushing. An interviewer once asked a priest who had been at the healing shrine at Lourdes for many years, "What is the greatest miracle you have ever seen in your long time here?" The priest answered, "The look on the faces of those who found they were not going to get well." It is such evidence that lets us preach with the full assurance of God's help.

True faith not only calls for courage, endurance, and growth, but also has to do with fidelity. True faith always manifests itself in works. Works, according to the Epistle of James, are the tests that divide real faith from a mere profession of faith. The model for true faith is Abraham's response to God's command to sacrifice his beloved son Isaac. Abraham is vindicated as a man of true faith when he manifests his faith by his actions. This does not mean that good works, objectively considered, necessarily indicate the presence of faith, but it means that where true faith is present, good works will inevitably follow. Obedience is the fruit of faith. Without obedience, faith is shown to be false. Jesus stated it like this: "If you love Me, keep My commandments" (John 14:15, NKJV). We are called not only to believe but also to be faithful to God. The faith that justifies is a kind of faith that inevitably results in a new desire for obedience and holy living. "Through faith in Christ, every deficiency of character may be supplied, every defilement cleansed, every fault corrected, every excellence developed."[5]

Faith involves living. It is more than professing and more than understanding theology. In the final analysis it involves commitment to the will of God. Faith has a content that fills the mind and grasps the heart to the end that a changed life is apparent. The end of faith is fidelity to Jesus Christ. This was the whole faith the jailer and his family embraced, for the narrative ends with a glowing testimony that they were "overjoyed at finding faith in God" (Acts 16:34, Phillips).

[1] F. F. Bruce explains "why they laid hands on Paul and Silas and not on Timothy and Luke . . . partly because Paul and Silas were the leaders of the missionary party . . . also . . . that Paul and Silas would be the most Jewish in appearance: Luke was a Gentile and Timothy was half-Gentile. Anti-Jewish sentiment lay very near the surface in Gentile antiquity" (*The Book of Acts,* p. 335).

[2] Ellen G. White, *Prophets and Kings* (Mountain View, Calif.: Pacific Press Pub. Assn., 1917), p. 175.

[3] Martin L. King, *The Strength to Love* (New York: Harper and Row, 1963), p. 107.

[4] E. G. White, *Prophets and Kings,* p. 260.

[5] Ellen G. White, *Education* (Mountain View, Calif.: Pacific Press Pub. Assn., 1903), p. 257.

4 BEREA:
REJECTION TO RECEPTION

"As soon as it was night, the believers sent Paul and Silas away to Berea. . . . Now the Berean Jews . . . examined the Scriptures every day to see if what Paul said was true" (Acts 17:10, 11, NIV).

Like the plays of Shakespeare, the dialogues of Plato, and a host of other world classics, the Bible is a sore spot on many a conscience. Many people, even out of a simple desire to be well read, feel they ought to have read it. At the same time, they have all sorts of good reasons they haven't. For one thing, there's the Bible's forbidding format. The binding is apt to be the rusty black of an undertaker's cutaway. The margins are cluttered with references to parallel passages, and the text is overloaded with guides to pronunciation and inexplicable italics.

And there are other reasons. One of them is that the Bible not only looks awfully dull, but some of it actually is. The prophets are sometimes very long-winded and have a way of sounding alike. Then there are all those *begats*. And there are passages of scriptural Sominex that even Moses must have nodded over, such as the six long chapters in Exodus that describe the tabernacle and its workings all down to the composition of the curtains. There are all those familiar quotations—and, thus, the sense you get that you know what the Bible is going to say before you read it.

If you're still looking for reasons not to read the Bible, there's no getting around the fact it is also full of things that even the greatest admirers wish were not there. There are passages that depict the God of Israel as being interested in other nations only to the degree that He can use them to whip Israel into line. There is Noah, the one man worth saving from the Flood. He rides out the storm in the ark only to get drunk in port and pass out in a tent, where his son Ham beholds his shame. Or take the book of Deuteronomy, which contains laws thousands of years ahead of their time, such as the one that says a newly married man is exempt from military service for a year so that "he can be happy with the wife whom he has taken," side by side with laws that would make Genghis Khan blush, such as the one that Israel is to destroy conquered peoples utterly, making no covenants with them and showing no mercy. The sublime and the unspeakable. The divine and the human. Again and again they go hand in hand through the pages of the Bible.

In short, one way to describe the Bible, written by many different hands over a period of 2500 years and more, would be to say that it is a disorderly collection of 66 books that are often tedious, barbaric, obscure; a swarming compost of a book; an Irish stew of poetry and propaganda, law and legalism, history and hysteria.

And yet, just because it is a book about both the sublime and the unspeakable, it is a book also about life. It is a book about people who could be both believing and unbelieving, innocent and guilty, crusaders and crooks, full of hope and full of despair. In other words, it is a book about *us*.

And it is also a book about God. If it is not about the God we believe in, than it is about the God we do not believe in. One way or another, the story we find in the Bible is our own story.

But we find something else in it, too.

The Protestant theologian Karl Barth, in his book *The Word of God and the Word of Man*, says that reading the Bible is like looking out the window and seeing all the people on the street gazing up into the sky toward something that is hidden from us by the roof. They are pointing up. They are speaking strange words. They are very excited. Something is happening that we can't see happening. Something beyond our comprehension has caught them up and is seeking to lead them on "from land to land for strange, intense, uncertain and yet mysterious well-planned service."[1] To read the Bible is to try to read the expression on their faces. To listen to the words of the Bible is to try to catch the sound of the strange, dangerous, and compelling words they seem to hear.

Abraham and Sarah with tears of incredulous laughter running down their ancient cheeks when God tells them they will have the son they have always wanted. King David dancing for joy in front of the ark. Paul stricken on the road to Damascus. Jesus, His arms outstretched between two crooks, with dried Roman spit on His face. All of them are looking up. And listening.

How does a twenty-first-century person, with all of their hang-ups, try to see what these Bible heroes are looking at and hear what they heard? Is it a task worth undertaking? If so, why? How do you read and interpret the Bible without tears—or maybe with them?

Our journey with Paul westward into Macedonia provides us with an example of those who took the risk and found understanding as they followed a definitive scriptural methodology of interpretation.

Paul, accompanied by Silas and Timothy, took the Egnatian Way (a Roman road linking the Adriatic with the Aegean) through Amphipolis and Apollonia and, a day later, came to Thessalonica, the chief city of Macedonia. It received its name from Cassander, who founded it in 315 B.C. and named it after his wife, a stepsister of Alexander the Great. After Philippi,

Thessalonica was the place the apostles chose to target with intensive evangelization.

As previously in Antioch, Paul was invited to speak in the local synagogue. He expounded the Old Testament scriptures on three successive Sabbath days, presenting the historic facts of Jesus' ministry, death, and resurrection as fulfillments of the scriptures' prophecies and predictions.

Here some of the Jewish hearers were convinced by what Paul said, but the majority of his converts were Gentile God-fearers. Among them were a number of women who were the wives of principal citizens. Also, one of the Jews, Paul's host Jason (see Acts 17:5-9), as well as Aristarchus and Secundus (described as Thessalonians in Acts 20:4), were probably converted to Christianity at this time.

However, as in the southern Galatian cities of Derbe, Iconium, and Lystra, the Jews in Thessalonica who did not believe the gospel and were under a pretense of loyalty to Caesar, incensed at the conversion of the many God-fearing Gentiles embracing Paul's message, incited the city rabble against him and his colleagues. By the time that the rabble assaulted the house where the missionaries were domiciled, the missionaries had succeeded in making their escape. It is probably with reference to this situation that Paul, some weeks later, wrote to assure the Thessalonian Christians that he greatly desired to go back and see them, but "Satan hindered us" (1 Thess. 2:18).

Paul and Silas got quietly away from Thessalonica and made their way to Berea, some 60 miles away. Here Timothy rejoined them. Here, too, there was a Jewish synagogue, but the Jewish community of Berea received the gospel far differently than did their coreligionists at Thessalonica. "The minds of the Bereans," comments Ellen White, "were not narrowed by prejudice. They were willing to investigate the truthfulness of the doctrines preached by the apostles." Rather than studying the Bible to satisfy their curiosity, the Bereans studied so "that they might learn what had been written concerning the promised Messiah." And as they earnestly and faithfully studied every day, "heavenly angels were beside them, enlightening their minds and impressing their hearts."[2] Their procedure: "they received the message with great eagerness and examined the Scriptures every day to see if what Paul said was true" (Acts 17:11, NIV).

How can we study the Scriptures with the same fervor and genuineness the Bereans did? What follows are some thoughts along these lines, together with some practical suggestions on how to read the Bible. But first, let us consider some interpretation rules.

1. Interpret the Bible contextually.

The Bible is not a *Poor Richard's Almanac*, with each verse a maxim that stands by itself. A verse can be understood only in connection with what has just been said, what comes next, and with the entire scope of the Bible. When we use a text to support an argument or prove a point, we have to be sure our interpretation is in harmony with the whole sweep of Scripture and does not rely on tearing the text from its context. All sorts of strange religious aberrations can come from a misunderstanding, misuse, or misapplication of even one text. The first use of chloroform in childbirth was widely denounced as unscriptural because the Bible says, "In pain you shall bring forth children" (Gen. 3:16, ESV). Fortunately, Dr. James Simpson, a pioneer in anesthesia, knew the Bible. Did not God, he asked, cause a deep sleep to fall on Adam when he removed Adam's rib in order to make Eve? God's obstetrical example seemed to answer the objections.

This example of building an entire philosophy on one verse demonstrates that the Bible was never intended to be used in snippets. That isolating a single Bible quotation is dangerous and irresponsible becomes evident when one considers the apparent verbal contradictions in the Bible. For example, God said not only "Man shall not see me and live" (Ex. 33:20, RSV), but also "Blessed are the pure in heart, for they shall see God" (Matt. 5:8, RSV). Not only "Let your light so shine before men" (verse 16, RSV), but also "Beware of practicing your piety before men" (Matt. 6:1, RSV). Not only "Work out your own salvation" (Phil. 2:12, RSV), but also "By grace you have been saved . . . not because of works" (Eph. 2:8, 9, RSV). Thus, by dishonestly using Bible fragments out of their settings in a misleading way, one can exploit the Scriptures.

2. Interpret the Bible comparatively.

One writer suggests, "The Bible is it own expositor. One passage will prove to be a key that will unlock other passages, and in this way light will be shed upon the hidden meaning of the word. By comparing different texts treating on the same subject, viewing their bearing on every side, the true meaning of the Scriptures will be evident."[3]

The law of comparison is one of the first laws of learning. Paul was clear on this matter when he exhorted, "These things we also speak, not in the words which man's wisdom teaches but which the Holy Spirit teaches, *comparing spiritual things with spiritual.* But the natural man does not receive the things of the Spirit of God, for they are foolishness to him; nor can he know them, because they are spiritually discerned" (1 Cor. 2:13, 14, NKJV). This is a corrective principle. It is important to gather together all that Bible writers have said on any given topic before drawing conclusions as to what the Bible teaches on that subject. If our conclusions concerning one passage are contradicted by plain, unequivocal statements elsewhere, then we may be sure we have misunderstood the author. Though a variety of individuals wrote the Bible, there is in it a unified authorship, because each writer was "moved by the Holy Spirit" (2 Peter 1:21, NKJV). We would not expect the Spirit to contradict in any book what He has already confirmed in another.

3. Interpret the Bible exegetically.

We are supposed to use *exegesis*, which means getting out of a text the meanings that are there; we are not supposed to use *eisegesis,* which means putting into a text meanings that are not there. Some examples: The benefits of early rising can be deduced from the text "Mary Magdalene came to the tomb early" (John 20:1, ESV). The prodigal son's destitution has been used to teach the importance of using money wisely. By enough text stretching, "Simon's mother-in-law lay sick with a fever" (Mark 1:30, RSV) could be used to support in-law relationships, health care, or the fevers of life. Interpreters and paleontologists practice the same art. By chains of implication, a scientist can find enough indications in a five-inch fossil to reconstruct a dinosaur. Some texts are related in that way, though not always with such rigorous logic.

The emotional power of Bible words tempts us to exploit them to give force to what we say. For example, Genesis 31:49 is used for an affectionate "mizpah benediction" on those who separate. In effect, what Laban is really saying is, "The Lord keep an eye on both of us, because we can't trust each other." The danger of distorting the Bible forces us to investigate with great care to see whether our texts mean what we hope they do.

4. Interpret the Bible analytically.

Many texts cannot be understood apart from the circumstances in which they were written. Most become far livelier when we know the occasion for them. Finding their meaning requires us to answer the five W's: Who, Whom, When, Where, and Why. (a) Asking "Who?" means asking about the life situation and personality of a person who uttered the text or of the author of the book in which the text is found. (b) Asking "Whom?" means investigating the persons addressed to discover their needs, prejudices, and problems. (c) Asking "When?" is looking into the historical situation and the course of events that led up to it. (d) Asking "Where?" means studying the church, community, or country to which the text was addressed in order to see how it applies to similar conditions now. (e) Asking "Why?" means asking the reason for what the text says; why did the author say it?

Now note three cautions in interpreting the Bible.

1. Interpret the Bible without inference.

What the Bible may *seem to imply* is not a clear enough guide in helping us arrive at conclusions. A parable teaches only its main lesson. The parable of the rich man and Lazarus cannot be used to show the conditions of the life to come any more than the parable of the unjust judge can be used to show that God's morals are poor (see Luke 16:19-30; 18:1-7). Jesus' saying, "If a man does not abide in me, he is cast forth as a branch and withers; and the branches are gathered, thrown into the fire and burned" (John 15:6, RSV) does not authorize the Inquisition. Paul's use of military metaphors (see Eph. 6:10-17) does not show scriptural approval of militarism, though it does show that Paul did not shrink from warlike terminology. Good hermeneutics requires us to determine what a Bible passage was intended to say to those who heard it first. When we make a deduction that points to something else, we are twisting the text too far.

2. Interpret the Bible without elaboration.

The Bible writings have great force by leaving out details. The stories in the Gospel of Luke are considered to be among the most perfect ever written, partly because they have no embellishment. How much more we would have told (and do tell) about the prodigal son, the good Samaritan, and the travelers to Emmaus. The Bible's sparseness indeed leaves wide room for the interpreter's imagination. However, some of these inventive images have been falsely accepted as Scripture. For instance, the Bible never says that there were three Wise Men, or that Jesus fell under the weight of the cross, or that Simon who carried it was Black. Christ cast seven devils out of Mary Magdaline, but Scripture does not comment on whether Mary was a prostitute. Interpreters may be allowed some dramatic license in describing action, or in character development, but they must never use what they have added to support what they want to teach. If they do present their own inferences as evidence for their own ideologies, they are teaching that their notions are the Word of God.

3. Interpret the Bible without allegorizing.

The Bible contains allegories and symbols. Leaven, fire, water, blood, serpents, and many others are expressly intended to be signs. But when we go beyond what the Bible identifies in symbols and invent our own, then we are forcing meanings on the Bible that were never intended. A good imagination can ornament texts with symbols the Bible does not authorize. For example, ecumenical enthusiasts interpret Christ's seamless robe as His intention for an undivided church. Some equate the fragrance of the ointment in the alabaster box with Christian prayers, whose sweet aroma wafts to heaven. The Wise Men bring to the infant Jesus the homage of Asia, Africa, and Europe. There is no limit to how misleading this can be. The problem with this approach is that it lets the teacher present his or her personal philosophy as though it were the Word of God. Sadly, he or she may not even know that he or she is doing it. In the words that Shakespeare put into the mouth of Bassanio in *The Merchant of Venice*:

"The world is still deceiv'd with ornament.
In law, what plea so tainted and corrupt,
But, being season'd with a gracious voice,
Obscures the show of evil? In religion,
What damned error, but some sober brow
Will bless it, and approve it with a text,
Hiding the grossness with fair ornament?"[4]

But how can we read the Bible to relate its messages to our own experience? Here are a few ways to read the Bible.

1. Read the Word prayerfully.

We obtain the wisdom of God through prayer. When we ask for God's help in reading the Bible, we are also asking for that reading to work a change in our life. Turning one's thoughts to God elevates the whole conception of how the Bible reading impacts the immediate where's, and when's, and how's that face us daily at home and at work. And remember, the Bible is not a manual in which to look up answers to our questions; it is intended to force God's questions on us and to give us answers we may not want.

Further, prayer enables you to be a channel of the Holy Spirit. The sort of help Jesus promised His disciples has not ceased: "It is not you who speak, but the Holy Spirit" (Mark 13:11, RSV); "I myself will give you power of utterance and wisdom" (Luke 21:15, NEB). Paul recognized that "we impart this in words not taught by human wisdom but taught by the Spirit" (1 Cor. 2:13, RSV). Thus, the psalmist can pray with expectation, "Open thou mine eyes, that I may behold wondrous things out of thy law" (Ps. 119:18).

Prayer involves listening to God, waiting in silence to hear the divine voice. "Be still before the Lord," the psalmist counsels, "and wait patiently for him" (Ps. 37:7, RSV). And again: "For God alone my soul waits in silence" (Ps. 62:1, RSV). Ellen White captures the essence of this silent waiting: "When every other voice is hushed and in quietness we wait before Him, the silence of the soul makes more distinct the voice of God."[5] This waiting is not passive; it is like standing on spiritual tiptoes, alert and listening. For it is when we are "still" that we come to "know . . . God" (Ps. 46:10).

2. Read the Bible personally.

Take a particular passage and study it, focusing on Christ's presence in order to receive a personal message from Him (see Col. 3:1). "If we come to Him in faith," Ellen White explains, "He will speak His mysteries to us personally."[6] Elsewhere she says, "Christ is ever sending messages to those who listen for His voice."[7]

Thus, Jesus is speaking "in the continuous present," as A. W. Tozer puts it.[8] Whatever your situation, you have a Guide; whatever your perplexities, you have a sure Counselor; whatever your sorrow, bereavement, or loneliness, you have a sympathizing Friend.

3. Read the Bible daily.

The Bereans "searched the Scriptures daily" (Acts 17:11). One may ask, why such regularity? A.R.P. Williams, chairman of the committee of Protestant scholars who prepared *The New English Bible*, answers: "The Bible is not a Good Book to be kept on the shelves and savored occasionally for little more than fine sentiments and rolling prose. It is marked 'Urgent, Immediate.'"[9] As in the physical world, so in the spiritual. Spiritual growth is contingent upon the ingestion of "our daily bread."

The Bible on the shelf is a far more difficult book than is the Bible in use. Those who have come to love the Bible will live with its perplexities and cherish its beauties. The Scriptures give us so strong and steady a sense of the presence of God; so warm an assurance of His help and comfort; so clean-cut a revelation of His justice, power, and love that anything that interferes with this—the Bible's great purpose of showing us the face of the Almighty—is either absorbed or thrust aside. Exercising this attitude does not mean blind faith; it simply means that when we know for ourselves what the Bible really is, we can live with our problems. Such is the necessity of daily exposing ourselves to and immersing ourselves in its message.

In urging the students at Oxford University to read the Bible, John Ruskin said, "[Make] it the first morning business . . . to understand some piece of it clearly, and your daily business to obey of it all that you understand."[10] Long after our daily reading, the Word of God is still coming into actuality in our life and thought. The daily prayer of George Washington is worthy of replication: "As Thou wouldst hear me calling upon Thee in my prayers, so give me grace to hear Thee calling to me in Thy Word. Grant that I may hear it with reverence, receive it with meekness, mingle it with faith, and that it may accomplish in me, gracious God, the good work for which Thou hast sent it."

4. Read the Bible with a plan.

You may find some of the Bible to be dull reading. Often a

person who starts to read from Genesis through Revelation will lose interest halfway through Exodus and find little of immediate benefit for the next 100 chapters. Exhortations to read the Bible are not enough to keep us committed. Instead, it is good to choose and follow a reading plan. A good start would be 50 great chapters. There is, for example, the vivid eyewitness account of the reign of King David (see 2 Samuel and 1 Kings 1; 2) and especially the story of how his son Absalom, the handsome, dangerous young prince, who of all his sons is the one David was never able to live either with or without, is killed in the battle. When the old king hears this, he weeps: "O my son Absalom, my son, my son Absalom! Would I had died instead of you" (2 Sam. 18:33, ESV).

What stuns us in these words is not just the choked eloquence of human grief still raw after 30 centuries, but their strange foreshadowing of the Galilean peasant who generations later was hailed with psalms as the Son of David and who died just such a sacrificial death as the old king could only dream of helplessly.

Or take, for instance, the book of Job. It faces, in all its starkness, the questions that still pose the greatest stumbling block to religious faith: If there really is a God who is both all-good and all-powerful, then why is there so much evil in the world? Why does a good person suffer when the wicked thrive? Why is a child born hopelessly deformed?

God does not offer a neatly packaged explanation in Job. He returns with rhetorical questions: "Hast thou entered into the treasures of the snow?" (Job 38:22). "Canst thou bind the sweet influence of the Pleiades?" (verse 31). "Hast thou given the horse strength and clothed his neck with thunder?" (Job 39:19). God does not reveal His grand design so much as He reveals Himself.

"I have heard of thee by the hearing of the ear: but now mine eye seeth thee," Job says (Job 42:5) and the idea is powerfully conveyed that this was somehow what Job, like the rest of us, had wanted all along: not a God who would show theologically why things are as they are, but a God who would show His face—not a homily but a hand to hold.

Among the other high points are those sections of Matthew and Luke in which Jesus gives a summary of His teachings in words and images that have haunted the world ever since. Try the one in Luke, because, as the less familiar of the two, it is apt to come through fresher: "Blessed are you that weep now," Jesus says, "for you shall laugh" (Luke 6:21, RSV). There is generally so little laughter in the Bible that, here in this crucial passage, it rings out with extraordinary clarity: the astonished, joyful, tear-stained laughter of faith justified, hope fulfilled.

The air in these upper altitudes of the Bible is apt to be clearer and the light brighter than elsewhere, but if you nevertheless find yourself getting lost, try a good Bible commentary that gives the date and historical background of each book, explains the special circumstances it was written to meet, and verse by verse tries to illumine the meaning of difficult sections. Even when the meaning seems perfectly clear, a commentary can greatly enrich our understanding. The book of Jonah, for instance—only two or three pages long—takes on new significance when we discover its importance in advancing the idea that God extends His mercy and forgiveness not just to the children of Israel but to all humankind.

Finally, consider this. If you look *at* a window, you see flyspecks, dust, the crack from a stone a vagrant neighbor boy threw. But if you look *through* a window, like Alice in

Lewis Carroll's *Through the Looking Glass,* you see the world beyond.

This illustration is similar to the difference between those who see the Bible as unreadable and those who, like the Bereans, see it as the Word of God that speaks out of the depths of an almost unimaginable past into the deepest places of their own hearts.

In conclusion, Berea stands out as a bright oasis in the dreary landscape of persecution. When Paul and Silas enter the synagogue, they find themselves in a new atmosphere. They find "men of nobler soul" than the dishonest cavilers and intrigues of Philippi and Thessalonica. What were the elements of this nobility? I suggest two:

1. Willing and unprejudiced reception of novel views. This spontaneous receptiveness springs only from the rooted love of truth.

2. Independent inquiry. The Bereans did not carry on a battle of notions with notions; they went to the sources, and they studied the documents and the facts. The study of the Bible is a right, a duty, and a profound science. Hasty generalizations and fixed opinions must give way to larger light.

The Bereans were commended because they inquired. Those inquiries led them to the Scriptures, to the searching of God's revealed Word, and to the certainty that came with the validation of Paul's message.

---

[1] Karl Barth, *The Word of God and the Word of Man* (New York: Haper and Brothers, 1957), p. 63.

[2] E. G. White, *The Acts of the Apostles,* p. 231.

[3] Ellen G. White, *Fundamentals of Christian Education* (Nashville: Southern Pub. Assn., 1923), p. 187.

[4] William Shakespeare, *The Merchant of Venice,* Act III, scene 2, lines 74-80.

[5] Ellen G. White, *The Desire of Ages* (Mountain View, Calif.: Pacific Pub. Assn., 1898), p. 363.

6 E. G. White, *The Desire of Ages*, p. 668.

7 Ellen G. White, *The Ministry of Healing* (Mountain View, Calif.: Pacific Press Pub. Assn., 1905), p. 509.

8 A. W. Tozer, *The Pursuit of God* (Camp Hill, Pa.: Christian Publications, 1982), p. 82.

9 A.R.P. Williams, in *National Observer*, Jan. 7, 1963.

10 John Ruskin, *The Works of John Ruskin* (London: George Allen, 1906), vol. 22, p. 537.

66

5 ΛΤΗΕΝS:
PHILOSOPHY ΤΟ CHRISTIANITY

"And Paul stood in the midst of the Areopagus, and said,
Ye men of Athens, in all things I perceive that ye are very
religious. For as I passed along, and observed the objects of
your worship, I found also an altar with this inscription, TO AN
UNKNOWN GOD. What therefore ye worship in ignorance, this
set I forth unto you" (Acts 17:22, 23, ASV).

Athens was not exactly on Paul's missionary itinerary. Once again he was the main target of opposition in Berea and, as in Thessalonica, had to get out of the city quickly and quietly. As he quitted Berea, he could see behind him the snowy peaks of Mount Olympus, where the deities of Greece had been supposed to dwell. Soon he was sailing past Thermopylae, where the immortal 300 stood against the barbarian myriads; and, as his voyage neared its close, he saw before him the island of Salamis, where again the existence of Greece was saved from extinction by the valor of her sons.

Silas and Timothy had been left behind in Berea but would later rejoin Paul in the city whose only prophets were poets, "The Eye of Greece": Athens.

While Paul waited for his two friends, he had leisure to walk the violet-crowned city and view its masterpieces of architecture and sculpture. Notwithstanding that 400 years had elapsed since its golden age, no one of ordinary taste and culture could stand in the midst of its glories without being infected by a powerful sense of enthusiasm for aesthetics. Not Paul. Only a feeling of intense pity and indignation moved him. Temples and images of pagan deities were no new thing to a native of Tarsus, but this native of Tarsus had been brought up in the spirit of the first and second commandments. Whatever Paul may have felt in the way of artistic appreciation, the beautiful city was "full of idols" dedicated to the worship of gods, which were no gods—for "the things which the Gentiles sacrifice, they sacrifice to demons and not to God" (1 Cor. 10:20, RSV). Paul was single-minded; being the new man, living a new life in Christ—this was his sole focus. It is no wonder that this purely pagan environment made him uncomfortable.

There was the Parthenon, beautified by the skill of Phidias and Praxiteles; there was the Areopagus, dedicated to Ares, the Greek god of war (called Mars by the Romans); there were the famous schools of philosophy by Ilyssus. On every hand were images of gods and heroes. Pliny says that the city contained 3,000 such effigies. Petronius, a contemporary writer at Nero's court, says satirically that it was easier to find a god in Athens than a man. The apostle probably walked down the Street of Hermes, where a winged figure adorned the front of every house, or along the Avenue of Tripods, lined on every side with notice offerings made by grateful athletes to the gods who helped them in the games.

The sculpture, literature, and oratory of Athens in the fifth and fourth centuries B.C. have, indeed, never been surpassed. In philosophy, too, it occupied the leading place, being the native city of Socrates and Plato and the adopted home of Aristotle, Epicurus, and Zeno. Heroditus and Pythagoras and Xenophon and Praxiteles wrote, chiseled, taught, thundered, or sang in this city. In all these fields Athens retained unchallenged prestige, and it political glory, as the cradle of democracy, was not completely dimmed. In consideration of its splendid past, the Romans left Athens free to carry on its own institutions as a free and allied city within the Roman Empire.

Yet even in Paul's day the living Athens was a thing of the past. "Philosophy had degenerated into sophistry," wrote Stalker, "art into dilettantism, oratory into rhetoric, poetry into verse-making."[1] It was a city living on its past. Aristotle, who represents the highest point in Greek thought, was not fortunate enough to have a worthy disciple to carry on after him, until Thomas Aquinas came. And so Aristotle's spiritual bequest to his people was wasted away by mediocre men. The Sophists threw religion aside and sought to see the divine origin of things in the interplay of atoms or in the inevitable force of natural law. The old ideals and models now became empty forms. The old Greek spirit drooped its wings and was no longer able to rise again.

Paul found no one of Plato's or Aristotle's stature; he merely heard the meaningless repetition of their sayings. With few exceptions, all of Greece's philosophers tottered about, leaning on the beggar's staff. The Stoics and Epicureans mentioned in Acts had themselves become that derisive thing, "word sowers." Deftly they draped the philosopher's cloak about their shoulders, but the prophet was not to be found under the cloak. Strangers coming to Athens were shown the academy of Plato or the plane trees in the Valley of Ilyssos, where Socrates reclined with his followers, or Aristotle's Lyceum, the Stoa of Zeno, and the Garden of Epicurus. They liked to promenade in the agora (a Greek city's central gathering place, full of life and activity), carrying little canes, their hands washed in perfumed water; here in the government buildings, in the bazaars and temples, they stopped to talk with their acquaintances and exchange some literary saying. They heard the news about any new mode in philosophy, politics, religion.

The breath of moral decay pervaded the atmosphere. Citizens and all comers alike had leisure for nothing more than to tell or to hear some "newer thing." Aristotle and Plato were long dead, and less noble forms of thought now ruled this city of discussion. And this degeneracy of thought showed that human reason was impotent to resist an absurdly self-seeking sensualism and an ironically passionate dead-end fatalism. Idolatry had exhausted its invention. Priests, sacrifices, shrines, festal days, were always in evidence, but ritual had lost its earnestness. This capital of aesthetics was still hopelessly unsatisfied and restless.

Paul was not accustomed to taking a complete holiday from the main business of his life. The spectacle of a city so entirely dedicated to false worship stirred him to the conviction that here were people who needed the gospel he knew. Athens afforded him ample confirmation of what he had already learned, that "in the wisdom of God the world through its wisdom knew not God" (1 Cor. 1:21, ASV).

In the marketplace, the lounge of the learned, Paul conversed with students and philosophers as Socrates had been want to do on the same spot five centuries earlier. But he found even less appetite for the truth than the wisest of the Grecks he had met. Instead of the love of truth, an insatiable intellectual curiosity possessed the inhabitants. This made them willing enough to tolerate the advances of anyone bringing before them a new doctrine; and as long as Paul was merely developing the speculative part of his message, they listened to him with pleasure.

Paul visited the Jewish synagogue, as well as the Ancient Agora of Athens, and held discussions with the Jews and God-fearers. The Athenian agora lay west of the Acropolis and southwest of the Areopagus. The citadel overlooked the whole city and was crowned with the magnificent temple of Athena Promachos, the guardian or tutelary goddess, and other public edifices of rare architectural beauty.

Among those whom Paul conversed with in the agora were philosophers of the rival Stoic and Epicurean schools. The Stoics claimed the Cypriote Zeno of the third century B.C. as their founder. The name of their school was taken from the painted Stoa Poikile (portico), where Zeno habitually taught in Athens. Their system aimed at living consistently with nature, laying their emphasis on the primacy of the rational faculty in man and on individual self-sufficiency. "The system may be described as a form of materialistic pantheism . . . in contrast to Platonic idealism on the one hand and Epicurean hedonism on the other."[2] Stoicism was marked by a high sense of duty and a spiritual pride foreign to the spirit of Christianity.

The Epicurean school, also founded in the third century B.C., held that pleasure is the chief end of life. More specifically, the pleasure this school of thought deemed most worth enjoying was a life of tranquility, a life free from pain and superstitious fears (including the fear of death). Though Stoics and Epicureans differed on some points, they agreed that the newfangled message Saul of Tarsus had presented was unreasonable.

At last Timothy and Silas arrived from Berea with good news about the church there. Paul was encouraged again and began to visit the agora, trying to engage men in a conversation about religion. When Paul went there, he immediately attracted attention because of his external appearance, his threadbare cloak that made him look like one of the Cynic wandering preachers, and his alien nasal twang about which the people of Tarsus were frequently derided.

The missionaries had no trouble getting an audience in the paradise of gossips and saunterers, with its shibboleth, "What's new?" Paul's quaint philosophy did not seem to fit in any of the known schools. His little speeches, they said, were a topsy-turvy of Oriental nonsense; some Attic wit nicknamed him the "word sower," a man who gathers unrelated things together into a speech. But somehow the fellow was interesting, and some believed he really was "a setter forth of strange gods" (Acts 17:18).

This expression, "a setter forth of strange [some translations, "new" or "foreign"] gods" requires some explanation. According to Plato, the Stoics, the Cynics, Seneca, and Epictetus, the highest type of man was one who had a deeper and more sacred knowledge of the gods, and these men were regarded as the messengers of Zeus on some special mission to the rest of humankind. Pythagoras, Empedeocles, Socrates, and Chrysippus were among such special, superior men. Among these genuine examples of *theioi* one could also find impostors, such as those charlatans and magicians to whom common people liked to flock. Paul had met such an impostor at the court of the governor Sergius. But in eastern Asia and in Greece, people were very drawn to the idea that certain men could be channels of the divine. Such "divine" men appeared occasionally in Greece and Asia Minor. They practiced voluntary poverty and renounced earthly comforts and possessions, all of which impressed the Stoics and the Cynics as special signs of close relationship to the gods.

When Paul went to the agora, he must have made an unusual appearance for people to speculate that he was one of these "divine" men and a "setter forth of foreign gods." He probably made no objection when they understood that he was preaching a new religion. He probably knew that they had no inkling that this prattle would some day obliterate their philosophy and overturn their chairs of learning. But it took four and a half centuries until, in 529, Emperor Justinian closed the school of philosophy in Athens by one stroke of the pen.

The Athenians quickly gathered about the apostle. Paul spoke to them of Jesus and the Resurrection, or as the Greeks would say, Jesus and Anastasia (the Greek word for "resurrection")—a pair of new deities. He who introduced a god into Athens was counted a public benefactor. Thus he harnessed his audience's attention at once. To know, therefore, more of this peculiar doctrine, they led Paul to the Areopagus. At this time the Areopagus met in the royal hall of the Stoa, where Demosthenes made his speeches. Here was a temple dedicated to Ares, or Mars (hence "Mars" Hill), in which a venerable body of senators, who formed a judicial council, also called the Areopagus, convened. It was before this august court that they brought Paul, not to put him on trial in a forensic sense, but to let him give an account of his "philosophy." The apostle was not speaking as if accused; he was merely giving information about his teaching to the city's highest board of education.

Paul stood up to tell the men of Athens about the nature of the true God. Earlier he had seen the altar "to the unknown god" (Acts 17:23). Several sources indicate that in Athens at that time, as well as in other places such as Pergamum, altars were erected to some indefinite, unknown god. Unknown gods were to be propitiated like every known god. Paul read the inscription in another sense, as an agnostic expression, something like "Who is God? Who can know Him?"

In a sense Paul read the Greek mind aright, for since the time of Socrates and the Orphics, the Greeks had become more and more convinced that the well-known, popular gods were only partial expressions of this great Unknown. While the Socratean school had identified the great Unknown with the inner experiences of the spirit, the Aristoleans had demonstrated Him from the external world. But they were succeeded by the Academy with its passion for skepticism, and the

Unknown receded again into the clouds. Since now the God of revelation remained nameless to the pagans and the Jews were not to utter His name, Paul took this indefinite inscription as the expression of a longing for something higher and better, as a groping in the dark for the true God. Paul was no student of comparative theology; he heard the cry of proud Greece for the hidden God, the *Deus absconditus,* just as he had heard the Macedonian's cry at Troas.

So Paul set forth the true object of worship, first, as the One who created the world, or in their own language, "the cosmos," with all the order, beauty, adaptation, design, and uses of all living beings in it. He is "the Lord," the Possessor and Master of heaven and earth. And being so great, high, infinite, and of almighty power, spirituality, and prescience, He clearly could not dwell in temples made with hands. Further, Paul went on to declare that God had revealed His moral character—as the God of righteousness—in the person of Jesus Christ. If He had overlooked the ignorance of the past, He would do so no longer, for He had "appointed a day in which he will judge the world in righteousness by that man whom he hath ordained; whereof he hath given assurance unto all men, in that he hath raised him from the dead" (Acts 17:31).

And yet, why did Paul defer the misunderstood subject of the Resurrection to the end of his speech (verse 8)? Mikeal C. Parsons comments: "This rhetorical strategy of deferral, known as the 'subtle approach' (*insinuatio*), was appropriate for controversial or difficult issues. . . . The sermon ends with God as the main actor: God overlooks, commands, sets the day, judges the world, and provides proof through the resurrection."[3] When Paul advanced beyond these preliminaries to touch the consciences of his audience and address them about their own salvation, they departed as one body and left him talking. Paul quit his efforts in Athens and never returned.

Righteousness was the ruling passion of Paul's soul, and as he looked around at that world of many gods and of much wickedness, his spirit was mightily stirred to declare to it a God of righteousness who would judge the world righteously. No wonder that the consciences of the Epicureans, who taught that expediency was the test of action and that "we are governed by chance" and "pleasure is the highest good," were stirred.

What, then, is this "conscience" that caused these philosophers to walk away from Paul? What false fears kept them away from the true God?

Conscience

What is conscience? Conscience is a judgment of our reason telling us that we ought to do good and avoid evil. That leads to the question What makes anything "good"? A thing is good if it attains its intended end and the highest purpose for which it was made. A pencil is good if it writes, for that is the purpose of a pencil. If we use our lives for other purposes than those given by God, we not only miss happiness but actually hurt ourselves. Life's supreme goal cannot be to get the maximum pleasure out of this life, because those who concentrate on having a good time rarely have it. Pleasure is only a bonus or a byproduct of duty. One does not eat ice cream to have pleasure; rather, one has pleasure because one eats ice cream. Our experience proves that we are most happy when we do not seek our own pleasure at all; the glutted, the jaded, the satiated are more miserable than those who live to serve their neighbors. Such altruism the Epicureans did not know.

Fame, reputation, a full safety-deposit vault cannot be the supreme goal of life either, because all these things are extrinsic to humanity; it matters little how much one has on the *outside* if he or she is not happy on the *inside*.

Everything in the universe has something in its nature that God implanted in it to make it attain an intended purpose. Chemicals combine in exactly the same way everywhere in the universe because God gave to each of them its own atomic weight and power to combine with or replace other elements. Scientists discovered this law and named it the "law of valence."

The plant kingdom has another kind of law, which, for example, makes an acorn turn into an oak as if there were a little architect working on the inside of it. Biology discovered these God-given laws and called them the "laws of metabolism."

Animals, in order to attain the end for which they were made, have instinct. All these things execute the divine will without knowing why and without being able to do otherwise.

But when you come to humankind, there is *reason* and *will*, by which a person can think out his or her final goal as well as freely follow or reject it.

The lower orders *must* be what they are. A primrose can never be a tomcat, but in contrast, people have no "must" imposed upon them; having an intellect and free will, humans merely *ought* to do something. This innate sense of "ought" is part of what we call a conscience.

Each of us has the power to regulate something *outside* of us. For example, Tom can throw a shoe at a screeching cat at midnight. But we also have the power to regulate something *inside* us, namely, to determine our character. Many things *happen to us*, but what is more important is what we *make happen to ourselves*. We are self-determining creatures, unlike frogs and stones.

Everyone appeals to a standard of conduct, even though he or she may deny it. It seems half an individual's life is spent telling themselves (or their neighbor) what they "ought" to do. Ants never say, "Get in line"; pigs at a trough never say, "Wait your turn"; bears never growl to other bears, "You would not want me to do that to you." Only humans use the argument "Yes, but I saw it first." There is no sense in saying anything is wrong unless we first know what is right. No referee could call a foul in basketball games unless there were rules.

This sense of "ought" in us, which is not mechanical, biological, or instinctive, but rational, implies a standard. Conscience puts before us certain principles to guide our actions. However, conscience itself needs help. We are all born with the power of speech, but we need grammar. Conscience, too, needs revelation. The Stoics refused to advance beyond the rational.

It is understandable that Paul's audience would resist any suggestion of a "standard" of conduct outside their own ideals, models, and abstract concepts of virtue and vice.

Salvation

Now, why did the philosophers retreat from any argument that intruded on their personal lives, especially any talk about salvation? What false fears kept them, and us, away from God? I suggest there are three: (1) we want to be saved, but not from our sins; (2) we want to be saved, but not at too great a cost; (3) we want to be saved in *our* way, not His.

1. We want to be saved, but not from our sins.

The great fear that many souls have of our Lord is for fear He will do just what His name "Jesus" implies, namely, "He who saves us from our sins." We are willing to be saved from poverty, from war, from ignorance, from disease, from economic insecurity; such types of salvation leave our individual whims and passions and concupiscences untouched. That is one of the reasons social Christianity is so very popular. Many contend that the business of Christianity is to do nothing but to help in slum clearance or the development of international amity.

This kind of customized religion is, indeed, very comfortable, for it soothes the individual conscience. It is even possible that some people who courageously participate in reforming social injustices do so because of the very inquietude and uneasiness of their individual consciences; sensing that something is wrong on the inside, they attempt to compensate for it by righting the wrong on the outside. Perhaps those individuals, who, having accumulated great fortunes, try to ease their consciences by subsidizing revolutionary movements, practice this same mechanism of diversion. The first temptation Satan presented to Jesus was to try to induce our Lord to give up the salvation of souls and to instead concentrate on social salvation by turning stones into bread—on the false assumption that it was hungry stomachs and not corrupted hearts that made for an unhappy civilization. Because some people think that the primary purpose of divinity is to relieve economic adversity, they go to Him in the moment of trial and then rebel against God when He does not fill their purses. Sensing a broader need for religion, others are willing to join a Christian sect so long as it concentrates on social "uplift" or the elimination of pain but leaves untouched the individual need of atoning for sin. At the dinner table, people do not object to a conversation on the subject of religion, provided that religion has nothing to do with the purging of sin and guilt. Thus many frightened souls stand trembling at the gate of bliss and dare not venture in, fearful "lest having Him [they] have naught [else] besides."[4]

2. We want to be saved, but not at too great a cost.

The God who dungs His fields with sacrifice to bring

forth the Vine of Life always frightens the timid. The rich man went away sad from the Savior because he had great possessions. Felix was willing to hear Paul only "at another time" when Paul spoke of judgment and the giving up of evil. Most souls are afraid of God precisely because of His goodness, which makes Him dissatisfied with anything that is imperfect. Our greatest fear is not that God may not love us enough, but that He may love us too much. As the lover wants to see his beloved perfect in manners and deportment, so, too, Jesus, in loving us, desires that we be perfect as His heavenly Father is perfect. As the musician loves the violin and tightens the strings with sacrificial strain that they may give forth a better tone, so God submits us to sacrifice to make us saints.

This fear that God's love will make exorbitant demands accounts for the many learned individuals who have come to a knowledge of God and yet have refused to venture to His sheepfold. The world is full of scholars who speak about extending the frontiers of knowledge but never use the knowledge that has already been acquired; who love to knock at the door of truth but would drop dead if the door ever opened to them. For truth implies responsibility. Every gift of God in the natural as well as in the supernatural order demands a response from the soul. In the natural order, people sometimes refuse to accept the gift of friendship because it creates an obligation. God's gift, likewise, involves a moment of decision. And because accepting Him demands a surrender of what is base, many become bargain hunters in religion and dilettantes in morality, refusing to tear false idols from their own hearts. They want to be saved, but not at the price of a cross; their lives echo the challenge to Jesus, "Come down from the cross and we will believe."

3. We want to be saved, but in our own way, not God's.

We often hear about the basic right that people ought to be free to worship God, each in their own way. This indeed is true, so far as it implies freedom of conscience and each person's duty of living up to the special light that God has given him or her. But it can be very wrong if it means that we worship God in *our* way and not in His. Consider a few analogies: The traffic situation would be tangled and desperate if we said that the American way of life allowed every person to drive a car in *his* or *her* way and not according to the traffic laws. Catastrophe would result if patients began saying to the doctor, "I want to be cured in my own way, but not in yours," or if citizens said to the government, "I want to pay my taxes, but in my own way and not in yours." Similarly, there is a tremendous egotism in those popular articles and lectures commonly entitled "My Idea of Religion," "My Idea of God," and the like. An individual religion can be as misleading and uninformed as an individual astronomy or an individual mathematics.

Individuals who say "I will serve God in my way, and you serve God in your way" ought to inquire whether it would not be advisable to serve God in His way. But it is precisely this prospect of a stable, universally true religion that frightens the modern soul. For if people's consciences are uneasy, they want, instead, a religion that will leave hell out of the picture. If a person has already married against the law of Christ, they want a religion that does not condemn divorce. Such a reservation means that an individual wants to be saved, not in God's way, but in theirs. In thus refusing to let vain desires molt, they miss the fight to that "love that leaves all other beauty pain."

If many souls fail to find God because they want a religion that will remake society without remaking themselves, or because they want a Savior without a cypress crown and a cross, or because they want their own blueprints and not God's, we are compelled to inquire what happens to a soul when it *does* respond to God. We can mention several effects, though there are many more.

First, a soul that positively responds to God passes from a state of speculation to *submission*. It is no longer troubled with the *why* of religion, but with the *ought*. It wishes to please, not merely to parse, divinity. There is a world of difference between knowing about God through study and knowing God through love—as great as the difference between courtship carried on by a computer dating service and one by personal contact. Many skeptical professors know the arguments for the existence of God better than do believers who say their prayers, but if these professors do not act on the knowledge they have, no new, additional knowledge of God will be given to them. They like to *talk* about religion but *do* nothing about it, and their knowledge remains sterile as a result.

A God-responsive soul, on the contrary, receives even a little knowledge about God with love; as a result, new portals of wisdom and love are opened. In such souls the love of God brings a knowledge of Him that in its certitude and reality surpasses the theoretical information of the professor. Paul speaks of this sublime truth when he says, "But if one loves God, one is known by Him" (1 Cor. 8:3, RSV). The woman at the well was an early skeptic: wanting to keep religion on a purely speculative level, she raised the question as to whether one should worship in Jerusalem or Samaria. Jesus took the discussion out of the theoretical realm by talking about her five husbands, reminding her that she had avoided making the moral amendments that true religion demands (see John 4:1-30).

Second, God-responsive souls think of religion in terms of submitting to God's will. They do not look to the Infinite to help them in their finite interests, but rather seek to surrender their finite interests to the Infinite. Their prayer, like the Lord's, is "Not my will, but thine, be done" (Luke 22:42). No longer interested in using God, they want God to use them. Like Mary, they say, "Be it unto me according to thy Word"; or, like Paul, they ask, "What wilt thou have me to do?"; or, like John the Baptist, they say, "He must increase, but I must decrease" (Luke 1:38; Acts 9:6; John 3:30). The destruction of egotism and selfishness so that the whole mind may be subject to the divine Personality does not entail a disinterest in the active life; it brings a greater interest, because the friend of God now understands life from God's point of view. Because of being united with the divine source of energy, a surrendered soul has greater power to do good. "If you abide in me, and my words abide in you, you shall ask whatever you will and it shall be done unto you. By this my Father is glorified, that you bring forth much fruit, and so prove to be my disciples" (John 15:7, 8, RSV).

Third, God-responsive souls move from a circumference to a center. The externals of life, such as politics, economics, and its daily routine, matter less, while God matters more. There is no dart in the quiver of a godly soul for anything but the divine target.

The truly God-centered soul is moved directly by the Spirit of God. There is a difference between a man rowing a boat and the same man being driven by a sail full of wind; the soul that lives by the gifts of the Spirit is swept forward directly by God, rather than by its own reason. Such a soul has a wisdom that surpasses all book learning, as was the case of young Catherine of Alexandria, who confounded the philosophers. It is endowed with a prudence and a counsel that is wiser than anything one can derive from one's own experience.

Divinely wise souls often infuriate the worldly wise because they *always* see things from the divine point of view. Is this the reason the philosophers of Athens chose to walk away? They were willing to let everyone believe in gods of their choice, but only on the condition that a belief in gods will mean no more than belief in anything else. They will allow the gods, provided that gods do not matter. But taking God seriously is precisely what changes behavior and makes the believer godlike. As Mother Teresa put it: "What is not God to me is nothing." This passion for God is called snobbish, intolerant, stupid, and an unwarranted intrusion; yet those who resent it wish deeply in their own hearts that they had the believer's inner peace and happiness.

The story of Paul's visit to Athens reveals the difference between the philosophy of the ancient world and the gospel of Jesus Christ. The circumstances introduce the speech, whose brief outline of only about 300 words is yet enough to show Paul's courage as a Christian and skill as an orator. Demosthenes and Pericles, Pythogoras and Praxiteles, wrote or chiseled, taught or thundered or sang, yet in my mind all those men and their teachings were eclipsed by Paul and the gospel he preached in this city. In most noble sentences he unfolded the great truths of the unity of God and the unity of humanity, which lie at the foundation of Christianity.

"Thus closed the labors of the apostle at Athens," wrote Ellen White, with "the Athenians clinging persistently to their idolatry," turning "from the light of true religion."[5]

Paul was no cultural barbarian; he was not an iconoclast. But his ideal was higher than the artistic ideal of beauty. His ideal was the beauty of the soul. He desired to form Christians out of living individuals, to make warmhearted men and women out of cold egoists, to form Christ in people's souls. In place of that beautiful myth of Pallas Athena coming from the head of Zeus, he wished to tell about the reality of the eternal Logos, the incarnate wisdom of God. Paul's was a far higher art than chiseling lifeless statues out of cold marble.

When Paul thought he had failed in his evangelistic effort to the Athenians, "he went out from among them," saddened and disillusioned (Acts 17:33, RSV). Did Paul fail? Parson concludes, "To view the Areopagus speech as a total failure would be a mistake."[6] Luke notes that while some laughed, others pledged to hear Paul again: "We will hear you again about this" (verse 32, ESV); and some "joined him and believed" (verse 34, NKJV). For, as he returned to his lodgings, he noticed that some people were following him. Turning around, he saw a dignified, friendly man who introduced himself as Dionysius, a member of the Areopagus who, according to a tradition reported by Eusebius, became the first bishop of Athens. He also saw a woman whose penetrating gaze pierced her heavy black veil. It was Damaris. There were others—not many—but they formed his little congregation in Athens. While the Sophists stood about on the steps of the Areopagus, ridiculing this unusual Jew from Tarsus, Paul sat with his new disciples in his lodgings and talked long into the night about Jesus.

German historian Ferdinand Gregorovius said of Paul's visit to this Greek city:

"In all the history of Athens, no event was more remarkable than the appearance of Paul. In all the annals of the Christian missions no action was more daring than Paul's sermon in Athens, the Acropolis of paganism, surrounded by all the brilliance of its arts and literature. From the meager report in the Acts we can guess what the inspired apostle told the philosophers of Athens: that this beautiful Hellenic world was going down to inescapable death because it was too narrow and loveless, because it rested on the privileges of race and the slavery of the barbarian races."[7]

Who would have thought then that this new religion announced by Paul in Athens would be the one palladium to which the Greeks would owe the preservation of their nation, their literature, and their language?

When Paul went to rest that night in his humble lodgings, what disturbing pictures raced across his mind? Perhaps he was in a mood like that of Elijah when the prophet sat beneath the juniper tree and prayed, "It is enough for me, Lord, take away my soul" (see 1 Kings 19:4). Perhaps some figure rose beyond the Saronic Gulf and stood on Acrocorinth, saying, "You have still a far way to go, Paul."

He was not able to found a large church at Athens. He never referred to the church at Athens in his letters, he wrote no Epistle to the Athenians, and on his third missionary journey he did not stop at Athens. Even in the second century, the church at Athens was not flourishing. Athens was one of the last cities to be converted; it was one of the last bulwarks of pagan philosophy against Christianity. In 529 (the same year that Benedict transformed the ruins of Apollo's temple on Monte Cassino into a monastery) the last seven Athenian philosophers, who were expelled by the edict of Justinian, wandered out of Athens to Persia to find refuge in the court of Chosroes.

[1] J. Stalker, *The Life of St. Paul*, p. 79.
[2] F. L. Cross, ed., *The Oxford Dictionary of the Christian Church*, (London: Oxford University Press, 1971), s.v. "stoicism."
[3] Parsons, *Acts*, p. 248.
[4] Francis Thompson, "The Hound of Heaven."
[5] E. G. White, *The Acts of the Apostles*, p. 239.
[6] M. C. Parsons, *Acts*, p. 249.
[7] Ferdinand Gregorovius, in Josef Holzner, *Paul of Tarsus* (London: Scepter, Ltd. 2002), p. 254.

6 CAESAREA: PROMISE TO PROCRASTINATION

"When the cavalry arrived in Caesarea, they delivered the letter to the governor and handed Paul over to him" (Acts 23:33, NIV). "Several days later Felix" "was afraid, and said, 'That's enough for now! You may leave. When I find it convenient, I will send for you'" (Acts 24:24, 25, NIV).

There was never a nation that produced sons more richly dowered with gifts to make its name immortal; there was never a city whose children clung to it with a more passionate affection; yet, like a mad mother, tore the very goodliest of them to pieces and dashed them mangled from its breast. Jerusalem was now within a few years of its destruction; here came Paul, the last of its inspired and prophetic sons, to visit it for the last time, with boundless love to it in his heart. But it would have murdered him, and only the shields of the Gentiles saved him from its fury.

Forty zealots banded themselves together under a curse to snatch Paul even from the midst of the Roman swords; and the Roman captain was able to foil their plot only by sending him under a heavy guard down to Caesarea (see Acts 21:38; 23:16-24).

Less than 40 years old, Caesarea lay almost painfully white in the brilliant Levantine sun, securely ensconced in a semicircular city wall. Herod the Great built the city at one time, a 12-year period from 25 to 13 B.C. It was named for Caesar Augustus and planned that it would serve as the center of the Roman provincial government in Judea. The Herodian kings and the Roman procurators had their official residence there. It was a matter of life and death for Herod to give the Romans a safe bridgehead. His subtle diplomacy aimed at (1) serving Augustus, whose eastern legions, after all, kept him in power, and simultaneously at (2) conciliating the Jews, his restless and resentful subjects.

Nature had molded the west coast of Palestine into a very rectilinear shoreline about halfway between Joppa and Dor. There was hardly an indentation in the vast extended beach to use in building a harbor. Undaunted, Herod the Great had created one artificially at Caesarea. By driving huge stone pilings into the sea bottom, he fashioned a great mole that was 200 feet wide to protect it absolutely from Mediterranean storms. Jutting up from this jetty were towers in which mariners lived while their ships were in port. Its position on the main caravan route between Tyre and Egypt made it a center for inland traffic as well.

Caesarea served as a showpiece for Roman culture. It contained an enormous amphitheater and huge temple dedicated to Caesar and Rome, featuring huge statues of the emperor. In New Testament times Caesarea was a mixed city, with Jews and non-Jews in its population. Pilate, the procurator of Judea, resided in Caesarea. In 1961 the Italian archaeologist Antonio Frova discovered a slab of stone from the theater bearing Pontius Pilate's name; it was fragmented and half obliterated—but obviously "Pilate"—and without accompanying titles or explanation. With the remnant of Pilate's name the letters IBERIEVM appear. Did Pilate, so eager to be, as the Jews sneered, "friend of Caesar," build the theater near a temple to Tiberius? Philip, the deacon, made his home there (see Acts 21:8), as did Cornelius, the centurion whom Peter brought to Christ (see Acts 10:1, 24; 11:11). Having escaped his Jewish enemies at Damascus, Paul departed for Caesarea on his way to Tarsus (Acts 9:30) and made the city his port of landing on returning from his second and third missionary journeys (Acts 18:22). Paul stood trial before Felix at Caesarea, where he was imprisoned for two years (see Acts 21:8). His defense before Festus and Agrippa also took place in Caesarea, and from its harbor he sailed on his voyage to Rome (Acts 25:11).

Paul needed rest. After evangelizing incessantly for 20 years, he required the leisure to garner the harvest of experience. In the solitudes of Arabia the influence of the revealing Spirit led him to understand the different dimensions of the gospel. Did the Lord permit his imprisonment so that he might penetrate more recondite regions of the truth? While Paul was in Arabia, God led him to understand that the destinies of the Jews and Gentiles had been tending to Christ's first coming. While in Caesarea, Paul arrived at the understanding that Christ is the reason for the creation of all things, that Christ is the Lord of worlds, and that the vast procession of the whole universe is moving toward a culmination in Christ's second coming.

During these two years Paul wrote nothing. But after his imprisonment, when he resumed writing, a more profound view of the gospel emerged. In the earlier epistles of Ephesians and Colossians, he builds on the broad foundations he had already laid down in Romans and Galatians. In Ephesians and Colossians he dwells less on the work of Christ and more on His person, less on the justification of the sinner and more on the sanctification of the saint. Another feature of these epistles is the balance between their moral teaching and theology. These epistles are divided into two parts: the first is occupied with doctrinal statements, and the second with moral exhortations. The ethical teaching of Paul encompasses the whole Christian life. A Christian life is marked by one's motives, which become manifest in one's conduct, and the supreme, reigning motive is to be a fruitful connection with Christ.

Antonius Felix, procurator of Judea from A.D. 52 to 59, began his life as a slave and lived the end of his life as a king. But Tacitus sums up Felix's career in the biting epigram "He exercised the power of a king with the mind of a slave." What wicked secrets lay hidden in Felix's conscience, we do not know; but the writings of Josephus fully confirm Felix's evil character. Felix was savage, treacherous, with a history steeped in blood. Whenever the occasion offered, he did not hesitate to employ assassins for his own ends, and "he himself was more hurtful than them all." His cruelty and rapacity knew no bounds, and during his rule revolts became continuous and marked a distinct stage in that seditious movement that culminated in the outbreak of A.D. 70, leading to the destruction of Jerusalem. His leaving Paul in bonds was but a final instance of one who sacrificed duty and justice for the sake of his own unscrupulous selfishness.[1]

The event that led to the introduction of Felix into the narrative of Acts was the riot at Jerusalem (Acts 21:27). There Paul, attacked at the instigation of the Asiatic Jews for alleged false teaching and profanation of the Temple, was rescued with difficulty by Lysias, the chief captain. But Lysias, finding that Paul was a Roman citizen, that the secret plots against the life of his captive might entail serious consequences upon himself, and that Paul was charged on religious rather than political grounds, sent him on to Felix at Caesarea for trial (Acts 21:31-23:31). On his arrival Paul was presented to Felix and was then detained for five days in the judgment hall of Herod, till his accusers could also reach Caesarea (Acts 23:33-35). The trial had begun, but after hearing the evidence of Tertullus and the speech Paul gave in his own defense, Felix deferred judgment in order to obtain bribes for Paul's release. But attempts to induce Paul to purchase his freedom failed ignominiously; Paul sought favor of neither Felix nor Drusilla, and during the frequent interviews he had with them, he took opportunities to preach to them concerning righteousness and temperance and the final judgment. The case dragged on for two years until Felix, being recalled to Rome for his misdeeds, desired "to gain favor with the Jews . . . [and] left Paul in bonds" (24:27, ASV).

Paul's defense was presented to Felix and a woman of extraordinary beauty at his side: Drusilla. Felix had made her his own by ruthlessly breaking up the domestic circle of another. She was only 18 years old, a princess by birth, the daughter of the elder Agrippa. She was Jewish by nationality. Felix had told her of the speech of the orator Tertullus, and of Paul's answer. Perhaps what she heard stirred her curiosity and she expressed a desire to see and hear this countryman of hers, whose fame was so widely spread.

The details of Paul's argument we do not know. No doubt, there was an appeal to the Jewish Scriptures, with which Drusilla could not fail to be familiar; he probably also appealed to the Stoic and Epicurean maxims that floated in the then atmosphere of Roman thought and could not have escaped the notice of Felix; certainly there was the intensity of a living conviction as Paul "reasoned of righteousness, temperance and [the] judgment to come" (verse 25).

Under conviction, "Felix trembled" (verse 25). Suppose his agitation should have passed at once into resolution. Suppose he would have said, "I will turn my back on my sins; I will be a new man and live a new life." But he did not. He appeased his corrupt self; he temporized; he played with his opportunity; he resorted to evasion, to self-deception; he excused himself and said, "You may leave. When I find it convenient, I will send for you" (verse 25, NIV). Oh, the well-worn, much-trodden path of self-excuse, along whose pleasant way thousands of travelers have gone on to their ruin. This is how we commit spiritual suicide, how we go to our death! We do not say presumptuously, "I will not"; we say feebly, falsely, fatally, "I will soon" or "I will when . . ."

There are three strong reasons we should not delay when we are under religious conviction.

1. Delaying a decision is guilty.

We blame our children when they hesitate or linger instead of rendering prompt and unquestioning obedience; but we are more bound than they to render implicit and unhesitating obedience to God. "I will when . . ." means "I will not *now*." This kind of response comes from a rebellious spirit in its least fragrant form, but it is still rebellion; it is a state of sin.

2. Delaying a decision is delusive.

We defer, imagining that we will be able and willing to do the right thing once we are farther along. It is fatal to reckon on this, because outward hindrances tend to become stronger rather than weaker. As our days go by, life becomes increasingly complicated, companions grow more numerous and urgent, and difficulties and entanglements thicken. The hedge about us continually becomes thicker and higher. Inward and spiritual obstacles become more difficult to surmount; the habit of the soul today is the finest silken thread that the child's finger may snap, but it will shortly become the strong cable that the giant's strength will be unable to divide. Well does Scripture speak of "the deceitfulness of sin."

3. Delaying a decision can be fatal.

If vice has slain its thousands, surely procrastination has slain its tens of thousands. For example, consider Caesar, who was on his way to the Senate one morning. Artemidorus handed him a letter that warned him that his enemies were conspiring against him. Caesar neglected to read it and subsequently was murdered. People who consciously and determmedly refuse to serve God know where they stand and what they are; but those who think they are about to enter the kingdom and protect themselves under the imaginary cover of submission and go on and on until they are enchained by their sinful habits, or until "pale-faced Death" knocks at their door, are found unready.

The wise man exhorted, "Do not boast about tomorrow, for you do not know what a day may bring" (Prov. 27:1, NIV). Those who boast about tomorrow are the ones who count upon it presumptuously and settle that thcy will do this or that, as if their lives were in their own power and they could ensure they would have time. This approach to life stems from blindness and arrogance. "You do not know what a day may bring." Those who feel boastfully secure about tomorrow act either *atheistically*, denying the divine control of life, or *presumptuously*, unreasonably assuming that God will aid their plans. Jesus gave a lesson on this matter in the parable of the rich fool (Luke 12), and an analogous warning based on this verse in Proverbs is provided by James (James 4:13). Furthermore, moralists and poets are always dilating on the topic of an elusive tomorrow. William Congreve wrote:

"Defer not till tomorrow to be wise;
Tomorrow's sun to thee may never rise."

Individuals who are confident without warrant are likely to be off their guard. Believing that all is safe, they do not fortify themselves against a possible surprise of mischief.

Deferring a duty until tomorrow may end up deferring it forever. A lost opportunity to do good is a sad sting in one's memory. *Now* is the acceptable time for ourselves and our own salvation. It may also be the acceptable time for others' salvation. How admirable to be numbered among those who, amid whatever pressure, can find time to listen, to comfort, to help others—today, at once!

We recall Haggai's denunciation of those who say, "The time has not yet come" (Haggai 1:2, NIV). The returned exiles were to reerect the Temple in Jerusalem. But they were preoccupied in seeking to secure material prosperity for themselves. They found the opposition they had to encounter as they engaged in the work daunting. Further, they had grown somewhat accustomed to being without the structure. Few of them had seen "the first house," not to mention a loss of that strong sense of the need of the divine abiding presence in their midst. Influenced by these considerations and forgetful that "good is best when soonest wrought," they kept postponing their duties and excused themselves by saying, "The time has not come."

The habit of delay is revealed, as in Felix's case, in matters affecting humanity's relation to God. In Eden, *"Ichabod"* became inscribed upon the once-consecrated spiritual man made in the image of God. Today the voice of God calls us to the glorious work of rebuilding this temple. In the life of Jesus, God presents to us the pattern we should imitate and conform to; in Jesus, God gives us the superstructure of a godly life and offers us His gracious aid so that we may build the noble materials of virtue and love into our character. It is precisely at this point that we are met with the temptation to delay. In this state of our relationship with God we are neither insensible to His claims, nor are we altogether indifferent about attending to these, but we say, "The time has not yet come." It could be that we are presently immersed in other matters; the cares of life, the pursuit of riches, the pleasures of life, absorb us. We are preoccupied just now, so we say, "The time is not come." We reason that the whole future is yet before us and that we will have ample opportunity in due course. So we go on robbing ourselves of "aspirations high and deathless hopes sublime." Edward Young wrote:

"Procrastination is the thief of time;
Year after year it steals, till all are fled,
And to the mercies of a moment leaves
The vast concerns of an eternal scene."

The moment the pressure upon us relaxes, we take advantage of it. People tend to put off unpleasant things until tomorrow, supposing either that the unpleasantness may diminish or that it may, by chance, be escaped altogether. And when tomorrow comes, "tomorrow" is again the cry.

There are two sworn enemies of the soul. Their names are Yesterday and Tomorrow. Yesterday slays its thousands. What it seeks to do is to plunge you down into despair. "You have had your chances," it says, "such golden chances, and you have trampled them all underfoot. There will be no more opportunities for you." But Tomorrow slays its tens of thousands. Brave vows and valiant promises that will never be fulfilled; good resolutions that may lull your conscience into sleep—these are its deadly weapons. "When I have a convenient season," it bids us say to the Savior. And how tragic that often the convenient season never dawns.

What are the reasons that influence us to say "You may leave" or "Go thy way"?

1. The natural wish to get rid of a disagreeable subject

Our dislike of "righteousness, temperance, and judgment

to come" leads us to make an effort to get our minds away from such contemplation, because the subject is painful and unpleasant. But when we recognize that something is wrong, would we not be wise to get to the bottom of it as quickly as possible to set it right?

2. The distaste of giving up something that we know is inconsistent with the claims of God

Felix would not part with Drusilla, nor would he disgorge the ill-gotten gain of his province. Felix was ambitious. He was unpopular with the Jews, but this worked in his favor in Rome. He might become superior. Becoming a Christian would ruin his prospects. "Felix," wrote Ellen White, "slighted his last offer of mercy. Never was he to receive another call from God."[2]

3. The tendency to let the duties and pleasure of the world crowd out impressions of the conscience

The weeds choke the seed that begins to sprout. When I am older and much less occupied, then I will have the time for secret prayer; I will then attend to God. Felix did not really intend to shut Paul's mouth forever, but he postponed his repentance. In his mind he would amend his ways at another time.

4. The inherent tendency to procrastinate and compromise

Remember the foolish virgins who found it too late to enter in? Remember the guests called to the feast who chose rather to look after worldly interest, only to be shut out from the kingdom? Remember the people whom Christ called, who wanted first to attend their friends and business, and with whom Christ would allow no delay? The intrusion of compromise works destruction in our spiritual life. "You may leave" or "Go thy way" are not only awful words, but may very well be the tragic farewell to God.

It need not be! Like the brave man in Bunyan's *Pilgrim's Progress* who said to him who had the book and the pen and the inkhorn in his hand: "Set down your name, sir!" At which there was a most pleasant voice heard from those within, even of those who walked upon the top of the king's palace, saying, "Come in, come in; eternal glory thou shalt win."

---

[1] See Josephus *Antiquities of the Jews* 20. 8. 5-7.

[2] E. G. White, *The Acts of the Apostles*, p. 427.

7 ROME:
INCARCERATION TO CONQUEST

"I must also see Rome" (Acts 19:21).

Storm clouds began to gather about Paul's head. We catch a glimpse of him in Corinth, planning a trip to Rome, when duty called him to the one place that was considered unsafe for him: Jerusalem. His churches collected funds for the impoverished mother church, and they asked Paul to head a delegation carrying the money.

He went to Palestine with grave forebodings. Hostility among the Jewish leaders there grew intense. When Paul entered the temple, a cry went up against him. Falsely accused of having smuggled Gentiles into the sanctuary—a deadly crime—he was jumped on by ruffians, dragged from the building, beaten, and nearly killed. In the nick of time the captain of the Roman guard dashed into the fury with a few soldiers and snatched Paul away.

It was the captain's duty to investigate. Paul was ready to lay down his life, but his fighting instinct told him to use every legal means to save his neck. When the captain ordered him to be flogged—the practice in interrogating a colonial subject—Paul calmly turned to the soldier, saying, "Is it lawful for you to scourge a man that is a Roman, and uncondemned?" (Acts 22:25).

A Roman citizen! There must have been a moment of stunned silence. No one questioned Paul's claim, but they escorted him to Caesarea, seat of the Roman governor Felix. As we have seen, Felix procrastinated for two years. But his successor, Porcius Festus, prodded by the Jewish high priest, held a preliminary hearing. Would Paul agree to be tried in Jerusalem, where the religious charges could be more easily examined? Paul knew his law: "To the Jews have I done no wrong. . . . No man may deliver me unto them. I appeal unto Caesar" (Acts 25:10, 11).

With that, the case was now out of Festus' hands. Having availed himself of his inalienable right, the prisoner was to be sent to Rome for trial by the emperor's supreme court. Embarked under guard and shipwrecked on the way, Paul finally arrived in Rome, where he was held under mild house arrest, "preaching the kingdom of God, . . . no man forbidding him" (Acts 28:31).

Paul had always thought of Rome the way a successful general thinks of the central stronghold of the country he is subduing and looks eagerly forward to the day when he will direct the charge against its gates. Paul was engaged in the conquest of the world for Christ, and Rome was the final stronghold he had hoped to carry in his Master's name.

It was not with the step of a prisoner, but with that of a conqueror, that Paul passed at length beneath the city gate. His road lay along that very Sacred Way by which many a Roman general had passed in triumph to the capitol, seated on a car of victory, followed by the prisoners and spoils of the enemy, and surrounded with the plaudits of rejoicing Rome. Paul looked little like such a hero: no car of victory carried him, he trod the causewayed road with wayworn feet, no medals or ornaments adorned his person, a chain of iron dangled from his wrist, no applauding crowds welcomed his approach, a few humble friends formed all his escort; yet never did a more truly conquering footstep fall on the pavement of Rome or a heart more confident of victory pass beneath its gates.

And what kind of Rome greeted his eyes? There was the capitol, the center of the civilized world. The standard of the Golden Eagle was floating over it, meaning that all nations had been subjugated. The known world, a narrow strip of land around the Mediterranean, with some provinces beyond, had been brought into abject submission to the nondescript beast in Daniel's vision, the beast with iron teeth, "devouring [and] breaking in pieces" (Dan. 7:7, NKJV). The Golden Milestone was now the center of the world. The Orontes had at length flowed into the Tiber, and "all roads led to Rome."

And there was the Pantheon, where were lodged multitudinous gods; gods of the fields and forest, of the mountain and plain. They had eyes but they saw not; they had ears but they heard not. It was all one to them whether there was light or darkness. How could they relieve the sufferings of humanity when they themselves were but larger men and women projected onto the skies? And the people had found them out! The gods had been put to shame by their own impotence. Plutarch says that the crew of a vessel off the harbor of Palodes heard the sound of vanishing footsteps and a distant cry: "Great Pan is dead!" John Milton, in his "On the Morning of Christ's Nativity," draws a picture of the flight of the gods:

"The oracles are dumb,
No voice or hideous hum
Runs through the arched roof in words deceiving.
Apollo from his shrine
Can no more divine."

And what was the condition of the people? Let us visit the Forum, which was the center of social life. Here there were three classes: patricians, plebeians, and slaves. Of the patricians there were 10,000 in Rome; they held all the wealth and culture in their hands. The plebeians were idlers, housed in tenements at the public cost. They hated work and loved pleasure; their cry was "Bread and Games!" The greater body of the population was slaves, owing to the custom of reducing subjugated peoples to bondage. There were 60 million of these in the empire. They lived in *ergastulas* (Roman buildings that housed enchained slaves) like beasts of burden, herded in stalls. Cato likened them to "cattle among the straw." These slaves performed all the labor—and without wages.

Now on to the Colosseum. Here were seats for 100,000 people. In yonder golden pavilion sat the emperor and his knights. The lower galleries were set apart for patricians and their households; then the vestal virgins; high up on the stone seats came the plebeians; and, last of all, freedmen and slaves. At the sound of the trumpet, a troop of gladiators filed in and saluted the emperor: *Morituri te salutamus!* They fought with one another and with the wild beasts. The sand of the arena was stained with blood. The dead were dragged out. The wounded appealed for mercy, but there was no mercy in the heart of the populace. To die, indeed, was better than to live, for "the world before Christ," says Gerhard Uhlhorn, "was a world without love."

David James Burrell writes in *In David's Town*:

"It remains only to visit the Necropolis, the City of the Dead. Here are gravestones inscribed 'Dormit'; but this is the sleep that knows no awaking. Death ends all. Cicero goes to the tomb of his daughter Tullia and, kindling a lamp, mourns as he watches it expire, 'O my daughter, is this the quenching of thy life?' Socrates drinks his cup of hemlock, saying, 'Whether to live again—I know not.' Read on this tombstone dedicated 'To the Eternal Sleep,' the words:

"'I was not and I became;
I was and am no more;
So much is true, all else is false;

Traveler, drink, play, and come!'

"The night had fallen; an unbroken night. The world was a world without God and without hope."[1]

This was the ancient "Golden Age" in which Paul was immersed. Art, science, and philosophy had done their best, and with this result: there was no clear vision of truth, no sound basis of character, no just conception of the rights of humanity, no social or industrial order, no prevalent charity, no real happiness, no thought of salvation from the shame and bondage of sin. The people were "walking in darkness."

Now Paul, in chains, entered the heart of the empire, and for two years and without apparent obstacle freely proclaimed the light of the gospel. "On this triumphant note, then," writes F. F. Bruce, "Acts is brought to an end. The kingdom of God and the story of Jesus are openly proclaimed and taught in Rome itself under the complacent eye of imperial authority."[2]

What happened next? Acts leaves us, at that point, without a clue. Many modern scholars believe that Paul was tried and acquitted. As early Christian writers tell us, he then went off on one more journey, reaching "the limits of the Western world"— Spain—and heading back to his beloved flock in Asia for a final visit. It was the height of Nero's anti-Christian fury. Now about 60 and world-famous, Paul was arrested once more and brought to Rome. Nero himself, tradition says, sat in the judgment seat clad in imperial purple. He was a man who, in a bad world, had attained the eminence of being the very worst and meanest being in it—a man stained with every crime, the murderer of his own mother, of his wives, and of his best benefactors; a man whose whole being was so steeped in every unnamable vice; he was, some said, nothing but a compound of mud and blood. And in the prisoner's dock stood the best man the world possessed, his hair whitened with the labors for the good of humanity and the glory of God. Such was the occupant of the seat of justice, and such the man who stood in the place of the criminal. Nero sentenced him to be beheaded by the sword.

Paul was "ready to be offered," and he moaned, "the time of my departure is at hand" (2 Tim. 4:6). These were his first last words. The old man, his hair whitened with age, his face furrowed with care, his body worn with disease and damaged by brutal persecution, was a captive in a miserable dungeon in Nero's Rome. The wretchedness of his imprisonment made him regret that he left "a cloak in Troas" that would have warmed him in the winter's biting cold or shielded him from the dungeon's perilous dampness. Still more keenly did he regret that he had to face his loneliness without the tender solace of his son Timothy's presence and the cheering companionship of his "books and papers."

With an unforced courage, Paul fronted his fate and looked death in the eyes. He could because he had "fought the good fight," "finished the course," and "kept the faith" (verse 7). This was no self-congratulatory note but an amazing example of what the grace and power of God can do. He was saying neither "I have been a good man" nor "I have made a good fight of it." The thought here has shifted from the apostle to the nature of his life and ministry. He was the champion of truth, purity, and liberty. Fighting against legalism in the Galatian letter, against impurity and sectarianism in the Corinthian letter, against idleness in the Thessalonian letter, and much more; till we find him in the Ephesian letter, charging people to take unto them the whole armor of God that they may stand and withstand in the Christian life. So here we hear the confession of an old warrior laying aside his weapons and putting off his armor in the final expectation of his reward.

"Henceforth there is laid up for me the crown of righteousness, which the Lord, the righteous judge, shall give me at that day; and not to me only, but unto all them also that love his appearing" (verse 8). What assurance! Paul did not always write this way. In earlier years he felt and expressed anxiety lest by any means, when he had preached unto others, he himself should be a castaway. And long after he "counted not himself to have apprehended" (see Phil. 3:13), he could only forget those things that were behind and reach forward to the future, still pressing forward to the prize. But now he had no misgivings. Why? Because in the solitude of his last trial, he had the assurance that when all human aid and human sympathy had failed him, his hope was in the Unseen and the Future. "And as the sword of the executioner descends," writes Ellen White, "and the shadows of death gather about the martyr, his latest thought springs forward, . . . to meet the Lifegiver, who will welcome him to the joy of the blest."[3] The climax of all was the triumphant look forward. So it is with those who fashion their lives, as did Paul, by faith in the unseen Savior in the hour of trial, and find consolation in that overpowering, increasingly felt Presence.

When is the "crown" given? Not at the day of his martyrdom but that of his Lord's appearing. So he looked forward beyond the grave. In harmony with the images of the conflict and the race, the crown was not conferred as soon as the racer reached the goal or the gladiator gave the final thrust, but was reserved until the contests were all over and ended and the claims of the several candidates were carefully canvassed and adjudicated. So the "crown of righteousness" is "laid up" to be given "at that day," when the Lord Jesus returns. And the "crown" is the emblem, not of sovereignty, but of victory. It was deserved because he "kept the faith."

Paul's personality was a strong one, and his determination was great. But the ultimate secret of his ability to *have kept the faith* did not lie in his own mental and spiritual resources. He kept it because he himself was kept (see John 17:11-15; 1 Thess. 5:23).

Life was full of voices urging him to give up the faith. Bribes and threats, beatings and imprisonments, and the constant whispers of the world had tempted him all along the road to fling it away as a worthless thing, but he kept it safe. He defended it by force of argument and against all that assailed it. But, above all things, he lived it and exemplified it in thought, speech, and actions. His doctrines are like the house he has lived in, rich with associations that ensure that he will never move out of it. His theology has been illustrated and strengthened and endeared by how powerfully it upheld his life; and no doctrine that has not done this can really be held up to the end.

The Christian life is not just the passive, reclining, restful experience that some have thought, sitting at Jesus' feet, leaning on His breast. That element is there, yes; but the battle is to get there and to keep there. "Believe me," wrote Samuel Rutherford to the earl of Lothian, "I find it hard wrestling, to play fair with Christ, and to maintain a coarse of daily communion with Him." It takes the whole of a man the whole of his time to be a Christian. The New Testament does not deceive anybody on this score. The strait gate, the narrow way, the much tribulation, the cross of which it speaks, as well as the hosts of darkness—all point to a strenuous conflict as the very condition of the Christian life.

The *crown* is not only the final recognition of the *righteousness* of the believer, but also recognition that the *crown* is achieved. It recognizes that righteousness is imputed and also recognizes effort. Even this is not the sole work of believers. They have to fight and strive indeed, but they know that their labor is not in vain and that thanksgiving is due God, who keeps on giving us the victory through our Lord Jesus Christ (1 Cor. 15:57).

Paul was not thinking of a special apostolic reward and

still less of a special reward for himself from which others would be excluded. It is for "all who have loved His appearing" (2 Tim. 4:8, NKJV). This expression does not refer to those who have ardently speculated about the date of the Second Advent, but to those who with steady faith have looked forward with joy to meeting the absent object of their faith and love. The perfect tense of "who have loved" suggests a steadily burning flame that has continued from its original outburst up to the present moment.

Alone in the dungeon, alone before his judge when "no man stood by" him, soon to be alone in martyrdom, he leaps up in spirit at the thought of the mighty crowd among whom he will stand on that day, on every head a crown, in every heart the same love to the Lord whose life is in them all and makes them all one. So we may cherish the hope of a social heaven. Humanity's course begins in a garden, but it ends in a city. The final condition will be the perfection of human society. There all who love Christ will be drawn together, and old ties, broken for a little while here, will be rebuilt in yet holier form, never to be sundered more.

"Beyond the war-clouds and the reddened ways,
I see the Promise of the Coming Days!
I see His Sun arise, new-charged with grace
Earth's tears to dry and all her woes efface!
Christ lives! Christ loves! Christ rules!
No more shall Might,
Though leagued with all the Forces of the Night,
Ride over Right. No more shall Wrong
The world's gross agonies prolong.
Who waits His Time shall surely see
The triumph of His Constancy;—
When, without let, or bar, or stay,
The coming of His Perfect Day

Shall sweep the Powers of Night away;—
And Faith, replumed for nobler flight,
And Hope, aglow with radiance bright,
And Love, in loveliness bedight,
Shall greet the Morning Light!"[4]

---

[1] David James Burrell, *In David's Town* (New York: Amererican Tract Society, 1910), pp. 30, 31.

[2] F. F. Bruce, *Acts*, p. 535.

[3] E. G. White, *The Acts of the Apostles*, p. 513.

[4] John Oxenham, "Watchman! What of the Night?"

CONCLUSION

"O death, where is thy sting? O grave, where is thy victory?" (1 Cor. 15:55, 56). The trial ended, and Paul was condemned and delivered over to the executioner. The aging challenger who had once sounded this rousing call to arms no doubt received the sentence calmly. He was led out of the city with a crowd of the lowest rabble at his heels. The fatal spot was reached; he knelt beside the block; the headsman's axe gleamed in the sun and fell; and the head of the apostle of the world rolled down in the dust. Three little churches, in a eucalyptus grove near Rome, commemorate the spot where Paul's head is said to have rebounded three times from the ground, causing three wells to flow. Some two miles nearer the old city wall, the huge Basilica of Saint Paul Outside the Walls enshrines a small memorial chapel built shortly after the apostle was martyred.

It would be another 250 years before Christianity became the dominant religion of the Roman Empire. But the decisive battles had been won. Jesus of Nazareth had founded a new faith, and the transformed Saul of Tarsus, having seen in it the redemption of all people, had carried that great new faith to far horizons.

"So sin," concludes James Stalker, "did its uttermost and its worst. Yet how poor and empty was its triumph! The blow of the axe only smote off the lock of the prison and let the spirit go forth to its home and to its crown. The city falsely called eternal dismissed him with execration from her gates;" but "even on earth Paul could not die. He lives among us today with a life a hundredfold more influential than that which throbbed in his brain whilst the earthly hull which made him visible still lingered on the earth. Wherever the feet of them who publish the glad tidings go forth beautiful upon the mountains, he walks by their side as an inspirer and a guide; in ten thousand churches every Sabbath and on a thousand thousands hearths each day his eloquent lips still teach that gospel of which he was never ashamed; and, wherever there are human souls searching for the white flower of holiness or climbing the difficult heights of self-denial, there he whose life was so pure, whose devotion to Christ was so entire, and whose pursuit of a single purpose was so unceasing, is welcomed as the best friends."[1]

So, as F. Scott Spenser suggests:

"Acts' mission story does not so much end as simply break off in midstream. Resisting its own intimations of Paul's trial before Caesar and ultimate fate of martyrdom . . . , the narrative leaves Paul with a hopeful future filled with fresh opportunity for vigorous mission. To be sure, there is a two-year limit to this scenario. But 'two *whole* . . . years' [28:30] is a long time, and whatever happens to Paul the prisoner after this stretch, we are left with a strong impression that the gospel of Jesus Christ which he proclaims will remain fruitful and unfettered. The missionary journey of Acts continues 'unhinderedly.'"[2]

Philip Schaff, the historian writes:

"The conversion of Paul marks not only a turning point in his personal history, but also an important epoch in the history of the apostolic church, and consequently in the history of mankind. It was the most fruitful event since the miracle of Pentecost, and [it] secured the universal victory of Christianity. The transformation of the most dangerous persecutor into the most successful promoter of Christianity is nothing less than a miracle of divine grace."[3]

The close of Paul's life is veiled from our eyes, but no cloud dims or ever can dim the splendor of the service of that life for God and humanity. He was indeed a conqueror!

---

[1] J. Stalker, *The Life of St. Paul*, pp. 135, 136.

[2] F. Scott Spencer, *Journeying Through Acts* (Peabody, Mass.: Hendrickson Publishers, 2004), p. 251. Note: Spencer uses the adverb "unhinderedly" to illustrate one of the two critical elements concerning how Paul conducts his mission: "with all boldness (*parresias*) and without hindrance (*akolytos,* unhinderedly)" (p. 250).

[3] Philip Schaff, *History of the Christian Church: Apostolic Christianity, A.D. 1-100* (New York: Charles Scribner's Sons, 1903), vol. 1, p. 296.